Manly Piety in Its Spirit

Manly Piety in Its Spirit

Robert Philip

Waymark Books

Copyright © 2023 by Waymark Books

This is a proofread and newly designed edition of a public domain work.

CONTENTS

1. Of Manly Views of Divine Love — 1
2. Of Manly Impartiality in Repentance — 17
3. Of Manly Avowals of Immortal Hopes — 33
4. Of Manly Views of Avowals of Faith — 51
5. Of Manly Devotedness to the Divine Glory — 68
6. Of Manly Estimates of the Evil of Sin — 86
7. Paul's Manly Glorying in the Cross — 94

1

Of Manly Views of Divine Love

Whatever difficulty or indifference we may feel about the duty of loving God supremely, we do not and cannot wonder that God should both expect and require us to love Him. It may at times vex, or even irritate us not a little, to remember how much love He demands from us; but it would both alarm and shock us if He demanded no love or refused to accept any from us. That would startle and stagger any man, however irksome he may deem the duty of loving God now: for no man could help seeing that a God who required no love would bestow no mercy. Indeed, the absence or the abrogation of the law of love would be ominous, even if we needed no mercy: for if God cared nothing about our hearts, it would be impossible to believe that He cared anything about our happiness, in time or in eternity.

We feel that we have hearts; and we find that nothing is really enjoyment but what lays hold of their affections. Whatever we cannot love, we cannot enjoy. We enjoy most what we love best. Did God therefore require no love, or refuse to accept any love, we could not resist the conviction that happiness after death must be an impossibility. For, from what could it spring?

Oh, it is the glory of both the law and the gospel that they claim our hearts and enforce supreme love to God. The requisition to love Him with all our heart, soul, strength, and mind may seem hard at first; but, were there no such law on earth, Heaven could not be expected nor hell avoided. Were we released from the obligation to love God, that very moment we should become identified with all the lost. Thus, we may well set ourselves to look into the requirements of the law of love, even if they were harder than we suspect; for you see at a glance that escape from them would be horrible. It is, I allow, against the grain of our nature to try to imitate seraphs or saints in their ardent love to God: but it is also revolting to our nature to level our prospects to the condition of Satan and his angels and victims. Accordingly, no man does so unman himself as to identify his lot with the devil. Even the devilish in character and temper cannot make up their minds to share the doom of devils. They are compelled by all the instincts of their nature to shrink from that misery, or to flatter themselves with the hope of escape from it, in some way. They either deny its truth, or take for granted that their "place" will not be with "the devil and his angels." Thus, if there is no natural tendency in man to emulate holy angels, in their present and perfect love to God, neither is there any tendency in our nature to bring down our future prospects to the state of unholy angels.

No man wishes or can wish to experience hell or be left out of heaven. You feel this through all your soul. You see beyond all doubt that you hate and loathe the lot of them who hate God. You could not choose it for your portion, nor be reconciled to it as your fate. The only thing you feel capable of doing is to hope that it is not true, or that you are in no danger. Which, then, of these hopes, is your refuge from the fear of hell? Surely not the former, for you cannot bring one proof nor shadow of an evidence that there will be no hell. All that you can do is to wish that there will be none. I do not forget that you can reason also against it. But, what are reasonings or wishes without facts to support them? And in this matter, the reasonings are weaker than the wishes. The wish that there will be no hell is prompted by all the instincts of our nature; but the reasonings against its truth refute themselves. Be not surprised at this assertion. It is not rashly hazarded. All the reasonings against hell are drawn from the goodness of God. And do you not see that whoever admits the goodness of God is bound to love God, and utterly inexcusable for not loving Him? If, therefore, you do not love God, you condemn yourself whenever you argue from His goodness against hell. All the argument upholds His claims upon your heart: and therefore whilst you refuse to give Him your heart, you are refuting the argument as fast as you utter it.

Be men: for it is worse than childish to hope in goodness which you do not love. It is both sheer folly and shameless effrontery to talk or think of throwing the safety of your soul upon the benevolence of a God from Whom you withhold the love and allegiance of your soul.

"Behold I show you a more excellent way." Give God your heart, and then you will have nothing to fear. Love God, and you are sure to live with Him through eternity.

Now, you wish to live forever where God reveals His glory, and dispenses joy unspeakable and everlasting. And, having this wish, what is the use of playing games of infinite hazard with a wish that there will be no hell? There is what is better, if happiness be your object: there is nothing but heaven to them that love God. And, do you not see that without love to God, heaven itself would be no place of happiness to you, even if you were admitted into it? You have often heard this. You know that this is the fixed persuasion of the pious. You may never have ventured to contradict the assertion. But, do you believe it? Have you never doubted its truth? Be honest!

You have thought that you could not be utterly miserable in heaven; however your heart stood affected towards God and holiness. You feel sure that you would be happy. You would take your chance (would you not) of any possible disappointment in heaven rather than go away into *the place prepared for the devil and his angels.* Now, I do not wonder at all this, whoever else may do so. I see the fallacy of your opinion: but I am neither shocked nor surprised by it. It is only the opinion I expect to find, in some form, in every heart where there is not cordial love to God and the Lamb. It is however, notwithstanding all its prevalence and plausibility, the most unwarranted opinion about heaven that can be entertained. Indeed, it is just as absurd, as if a man who had lost all appetite, or who was sick to death, should maintain that a sumptuous banquet would make him happy. It could only increase his sufferings if he were really in such a state as to loathe food. Nowhere could he be more out of his element than where the banquet was most abundant and luxurious. Nothing but the return of a healthy appetite could make such a table even bearable to him. Just so is the case in regard to the soul: if it loathe holiness, worship, and spiritual things, it would and must be out of its element in heaven: for there all the engagements and the enjoyments are entirely spiritual, and will be eternally spiritual. Nothing, therefore, could be made of them as means of happiness without a spiritual taste. And, as to their power of producing taste, by their own influence upon the soul, it is useless to speculate about it. That power can never be put to the trial, whatever it be: for, without both love and likeness to God, no man can enter heaven. "This is the Law of the House." And it is a just law. For, now that both love and likeness to God may be surely obtained in answer to prayer, because both have been amply provided for by the free gift of an atoning Savior and the faithful promise of a sanctifying Spirit, it would be injustice to the Redeemer and to the Sanctifier to try upon any man who neglected them the transforming force of Heaven's natural influence. It never will be tried in order to change hearts that resist the Holy Spirit. It never will be tried to win hearts that stand out against the love of Christ. It never ought to be tried upon those who trifle with the blood of the Lamb, and the grace of the Spirit.

Crowns of glory with all their splendor; harps of gold with all their music; palms of victory with all their majesty; mansions of bliss with all their beauty; thrones of light with all their sublimity; yea, angelic fellowship with all its sweet influence, ought not to be brought to bear upon minds which have braved all the attractions of the cross, and broken through all the restraints of the gospel.

No; heaven itself must not be put above the Savior or the Sanctifier. Indeed, it would answer no good purpose even if the experiment were fully tried. For, who that thinks for a moment and does not see that if the scenery, the society, or the glories of heaven could have won man back to the love and likeness of God, at however distant a period, or by however slow degrees, that God would have preferred that cheap plan of saving to the costly scheme of giving His Son to the cross, and his Spirit to the church? Immanuel left heaven, and the eternal Spirit works on earth just because heaven with all its charms could not convert the soul to God. This is no speculation, no hasty assertion. Remember ye not that Satan and his angels fell from the love and image of God, in the very midst and meridian of heaven's glories: How then could scenes or society which failed to keep pure spirits holy, restore or renew impure spirits? Thus, if there be nothing more plausible, there is nothing more hollow than the supposition that admission to heaven would be accompanied with holy effects. And, it is no reflection upon either its character or influence to proclaim that "the Heaven of Heavens" could not win nor wean a soul from sin which the cross had failed to conquer. There is, then, the very same reason for keeping them who love not God out of heaven as for expelling from it those angels who ceased to love Him.

Those who have not begun to love God nor to try to love Him are just as unfit for His presence as those who have left off loving Him. It is, indeed, mortifying, as well as painful, to admit this humiliating fact in our own case: but the conclusion is inevitable. We cannot avoid seeing and feeling that there is a gross and glaring inconsistency between the hope of living forever with God, and the consciousness of not loving God. Notwithstanding all our selfishness and partiality, we must acknowledge it to be both unnatural and improbable that God could admit any soul to dwell in his temple that had no love for His service or salvation, his character or authority. Thus it is—that the dread anathema of Scripture against those who love not God and the Lamb finds some echo in our own consciences whenever we allow ourselves to reflect seriously. Now, it is by such considerations that the general sense of the duty and necessity of loving God is kept alive in our minds. Accordingly we do not even think of denying or questioning His right to the supreme affection of our hearts. Indeed, admitting the right—is one of the ways in which we try to palliate our want of love to God. We compliment the duty as an apology for not complying with it. We express regret for loving Him so little, in the hope that the regret will pass as an excuse for not trying to love Him more. Thus we entrench ourselves in the abuse maxim—that God will "take the will for the deed," seeing we do not deny the duty. There are, however, times in our lot and experience, when this process is felt to be equally fallacious and unsafe. We occasionally awake to the absurdity and criminality of trying to find excuses for not loving "the God with whom we have to do." We see, and cannot help seeing that it is base as well as foolish to evade the law of love: for, to get rid of that obligation would be to rush into the "chains of darkness," where God neither loves, nor accepts of love!

But then comes the question, how shall we acquire love to God? It is proper, necessary, and indispensable to love Him, if we would live with Him: but how can we produce such love as God requires? Our hearts do not naturally yield it; and they cannot be forced into it. Love will not be forced, whatever else may be extorted. You feel this. So do I. Accordingly when we pause and say to ourselves, however solemnly,–" I must love God;" no love follows this solemn charge. The heart flutters with a keen sense of duty; but there is no rising of cordial affection in it. Even when we charge our souls by all the warnings of final judgment, to love; fear, not love, springs up in the heart. We feel none of those warm and tender emotions towards God, which we are conscious of towards our earthly friends. We find that we cannot give our hearts to Him so freely as we give them to temporal things. Thus even when we try to love God by this process, we are compelled to confess that "we can make nothing of it." We actually discover that the more we see the absolute necessity of loving God supremely, the more we feel the utter impossibility of doing so by this method of attempting the duty.

In this dilemma, we try to salve up the matter by the fond hope that our hearts will take some happy turn in course of time and come round of themselves to a better spirit: or, we hope that some happy event of grace or providence will occur to set them right. Having heard that "the love of God is shed abroad in the heart by the Holy Ghost," we also propose to ourselves to wait for the work of the Spirit. And a strange kind of waiting it is. We wait for the Spirit, without waiting on the Spirit, by meditation and prayer. What is the consequence? The Spirit does not produce love to God. Even the occasional cry

"Kindle a flame of sacred love, In these cold hearts of ours," brings no change of heart. Year after year passes away in this vague hoping and vapid wishing; but our hearts neither become as "live coals," nor as "smoking flax."

Do consider this experimental fact. You know something of this idle and aimless waiting for divine influence. Is it not utterly useless? Could it have defeated itself, or disappointed you, more completely, if you had been waiting for the gift of prophecy or miracles? You pity and blame the visionaries of our times who have been "mouthing the heavens" with clamorous outcries for miraculous and prophetic power. It is, however, much wiser, or more warranted, to wait for the grace of the Spirit! How can prayerlessness look for His "sacred fire," to warm or renew the heart? You got hold of a glorious principle, when, after trying in vain to force your hearts to love God, you began to think of the agency of the Holy Spirit: but you took hold of this principle at the wrong end. You left the matter to the Spirit, instead of looking to Him with solicitude and supplication. You gave up the work yourself, but you did not place it in His hands, pleading that He would shed abroad the love of God in your heart. This is both a sad and sinful oversight. And it is not the only oversight you have been guilty of since you were convinced of the necessity and propriety of loving God supremely. You have overlooked also, the revealed and experimental fact that the Holy Spirit works by means, and wins the heart by motives, adapted to produce love to God. He does not kindle love as by a magical charm; nor dart His sacred fire into the soul as the electric bolts of heaven penetrate the mines of the earth; and by a sudden stroke of concentrated heat transform its minerals into blazing gems. No; it is not even by direct impulses on the heart that He changes the heart from coldness to warmth; from stone to flesh: but by bringing some divine truth to bear with divine power upon the heart.

The Spirit leads men to love God by leading them to study, understand, and believe the love of God to man. It is thus, He "directs their hearts unto the love of God." According to "the Ministry of the Spirit," love begets love. Accordingly the primitive explanation of the whole matter was, *"We love Him, because He first loved us."* And you never can love God as the primitive Christians did, nor indeed love Him at all, until like them you set yourselves to *"know and believe the love wherewith God hath loved us."*

We are however naturally inclined to suspect that God feels no particular love toward us. We suppose that He only cares for us in the proportion that we care for Him: and as that is very little, we do not see in Him love enough to beget love in us. Indeed, God seems to us rather a hard Master than a tender Father. His great object is, as we think (whilst we think without the Gospel), to restrain us from our pleasures, and to cross our inclinations. We feel as if He delighted chiefly in marking and remembering and denouncing our faults. Accordingly, we do not like to think of God nor to retain Him in our knowledge. It is a painful subject in general, to us. Even when we hear it proved that *"God is love;"* and when referred to the demonstration of this fact in the gift of His Son as an atoning sacrifice, we are not at once convinced, nor much gratified. For, we have heard too, that sovereignty is the rule of His love, as well as that sacrifice is the medium of it; and as we do not know that we are "chosen unto salvation," we suspect the worst at times and, in general, feel as if success in seeking salvation were a very doubtful thing in our own case. This readiness to fasten upon the sovereignty of God as a reason for questioning the love of God, or as a hindrance to loving Him, is a remarkable but melancholy feature of our natural character. The Divine sovereignty ought to have just the opposite effect upon our minds: for it is both intended and calculated to endear the love of God to us, and to win our love to Him. Does this assertion surprise you at all? It certainly ought not to do so. Nothing is more capable of proof, yea, of demonstration, than the fact, that the sovereignty of Divine love is the first ground of human hope. God must love, according to some rule, and for some reason.

Now, we can find no reason in ourselves why He should love us. We can find plenty of reasons, both in our character and spirit, why He might justly hate us. For, what else, or less, do we deserve: It is, indeed, humiliating to admit that we deserve no love from the Father of our Spirits; but it is impossible to deny the fact that we have done nothing to merit or win His love. We may so far forget His revealed character as to think His anger too severe; but we cannot so far forget our own conduct as to think that we deserve His love. By no ingenuity of sophistry or selfishness could we make out, from our hearts or history, the shadow of a claim upon the love of God.

Thus, His love cannot find its reasons in us: for we cannot find them in ourselves. Unless, therefore, God finds reasons in Himself for loving us, there is no hope for us. We therefore are certainly not the persons to whom the sovereignty of His love should be either offensive or appalling. We ought to be delighted, yea transported, with the fact that God loves *"according to the counsel and good pleasure of His own will;"* and thus finds reasons in Himself for caring more about man than man cares about Him. Thus, the sovereignty of divine love may become the anchor of the soul when the other characteristics of that love fail to overcome our fears and suspicions.

Reconsider this fact. It will bear examination, and repay study. Now, unless we can obtain an interest in the love of God, nothing else we could obtain from Him would avail for our salvation. There is neither mercy nor grace for any creature for whom God has no love. Where He does not love at all, He does not save at all. Seeing, then, that we can find nothing in ourselves which deserves, or is likely to win, His love, well may we hail with hallelujahs of wonder and gratitude the glorious fact that God can find in Himself, and in the mediation of Christ, and in the final ends of His moral government, reasons for loving sinners! Here we can come in, although we have nothing to say for ourselves. This meets our case, whatever we be. Divine love is sovereign love, which finds both its rule and all its first reasons in itself, and not in its objects. The question of obtaining an interest in it comes, therefore, to this one point—can we do anything else, or anything better than to cast ourselves upon the good will of God to man? That is, indeed sovereign; but it is something—it is much—it is enough, to encourage prayerful hope; whereas, there is nothing at all in ourselves to warrant hope in God.

The choice is, therefore, between something and nothing! If, therefore, the something were far less than it is, it is, in a case of eternal life or death, infinitely better than nothing. Now, I repeat, and you feel that we have absolutely nothing in ourselves to merit the love of God. We cannot assign or conceive one reason why He should love us for our own sake. This, then, is our condition, whilst we stand upon our own character, before God. But, the moment we quit that untenable ground, and take our stand upon the revealed character of God as Love, we have in that all that anyone has to encourage a good hope through grace. Yes; all that anyone has! For, what have the best to warrant hope, but just the character of "God in Christ"? And, if we cannot trust to that, then there is nothing in the universe trustworthy.

I am neither mystifying you nor getting beyond my own depth, in this matter. I am as ignorant as you can be of all the secret purposes of Jehovah. The only thing I know of them is that they were "purposed in Christ;" for the sake of Christ; for the glory of Christ; and for the sake and glory of Christ as a Savior; and, therefore, they cannot falsify the word of Christ; which is, that, "whosoever cometh, He will in nowise cast out." This, I am aware leaves the sovereignty of divine love, just where it was. True: and, where else would you have it: You cannot wish that it were away altogether: for that would be to wish that all God's own godlike reasons, and motives, and ends, for loving man, were taken away. We have something to look up to and to rely on in love that can find both its first cause and its final glory in the gratification of its own sympathies: but we have nothing to hope for, if we ourselves must furnish a title to the love of God before we can obtain an interest in it.

Thus, they do not know what they are about, who take offence at the sovereignty of God. It is His own personal reason for all the love He bears to His enemies. And, how strong a reason it is to Himself, let the gift of His Son and the promise of His Spirit prove to you, illustrate to you; let the permanency and pathos of the ministry of reconciliation on earth attest to you.

This, then, is the character of the God with whom we have to do. This God of love is the God who claims our love to Himself. Now, meet fairly the question—can you love this God Remember? He can find reasons in Himself, and reasons in the cross, and reasons in the grand end of all His works, for loving you with an everlasting love; for, in those moving and meritorious causes, God has found all His first reasons for all the love which He has ever shown to any one; and, in these causes, He will find the reasons of all the love which He will continue to show from henceforth. You, therefore, stand in the very same relation to these originating causes of divine love as that in which patriarchs stood before they were called; as that in which prophets and apostles stood before they were inspired as that in which all the general assembly of the church of the first-born in heaven stood, before they were converted. God does not, therefore, claim your love to Himself, without, or before, giving you strong reasons for loving Him. No, indeed: He gives you all the encouragements, He ever gave to any one, since the time that love began to be claimed from man, by the ordinary means of grace.

Can you, then, ask or wish more encouragement than this? It is all that others have. Unless, therefore, your soul be more valuable than theirs; or your love of more importance to God than their love is, why should you obtain more encouragement than others? I know not, of course, how you feel, in the grasp of this question; but I feel that it brings a hot blush into my own face. It summons up recollections of a craving curiosity, and of a presumptuous humor, which amounted to little less than dictating to God the terms on which, alone, I would love Him. But I now see that if I had even less encouragement than others, it could not be too little to deserve my love: for the least is more than

I deserve; and any encouragement from a God who can neither mock nor deceive ought to be enough to win the heart of any man at once.

Oh, we forget ourselves, and trifle with our eternal interests, and tamper with the patience of God, when we cavil or quibble with the mysteries of His good will towards man. Such pettish and prying humors ill become those who must confess that neither their character nor spirit presents one winning point of moral attraction to the eye or the heart of God. Even a shadow of hope, or the barest possibility of salvation, ought to entrance our souls so entirely that they could not rest until they had yielded up all their affections and confidence to God. We are not thoroughly in earnest about their salvation, nor fully alive to their value, whilst we can object or hesitate to trust them upon even a "peradventure," from the lips of a "God that cannot lie." I know that their value should make us look well to the validity of the warrant for hope: but I also remember that any kind or degree of warrant from His lips is worthy of all acceptation by our hearts. Were, therefore, God's "Peradventure" the only cord of love that hangs from the eternal throne; the only "horn" on the high altar of the atonement; the only plank in the gulf-stream of time—I would lay hold of it with the death-grasp of a drowning man, and keep hold of it as the anchor of my soul until I knew the worst, or got hold of something better. And, if you would not thus venture your soul for eternity upon a divine peradventure—I doubt much, if it be yet committed to anything so trustworthy. Indeed, it certainly is not, unless you have already committed it into the hands of Christ; and there—more than peradventures guaranty the safety of the soul. For, in Him, all the warrants to hope are great and precious promises; and in Him none of these promises are "yea and nay;" but all "yea and amen, to the glory of God." No man, however, either will or can come to Christ to commit his soul into His hands for eternal safety, unless " the Father draw him " and, as the Father draws men by " the cords of love," or the loveliness and tenderness of His own paternal character, as the God of salvation, I want you to place yourself amongst these drawing cords, that they may have a fair opportunity of laying hold upon your attention and heart. For, whilst you overlook these cords of love, by which the Father draws the heart; or keep yourself far away from their reach; or feel afraid to lay hold of them, when they are brought near to you—how can they draw you? I mean, you have neither right nor reason to expect to be drawn by the Father, apart from placing yourself within the defined sphere of His saving attractions.

Remember how the Son explains the drawings of the Father. The Savior does not lead away our attention from means to mysticism; nor leave us to pour over a "chapter of accidents;" nor tell us to wait in ease and idleness until we feel the magnetic spell of love come over our spirits, like a magic charm. No; He tells us plainly that the Father draws by teaching. "They shall all be taught of God." And, that this divine teaching may not be supposed to supersede or set aside attention or docility on our part, He immediately adds, that it is the man who hath "heard and learned of the Father, that cometh unto Him." Thus, this "truth, as it is in Jesus," is, that the Father draws by teaching those who hear and learn of Him.

Now the great lesson taught by God throughout all His oracles is that He is a Father. This is always expressed or implied in every claim that He makes upon our hearts. Even when He demands our love by positive law, His own paternal love breathes in the claim, thus; "Thou shalt love the Lord thy God with all thine heart." And, when He condescends to entreat and beseech us, the Father breathes and burns in His solicitations; "My son, give Me thy heart."

Now, I want you to meet the claim of God upon this general ground, first, that thus you may be prepared to meet it, without suspicion or evasion, upon the special and splendid ground of the atonement. I would have preferred to have taken you there at once; and without any prefatory appeal to law or heaven, to have laid my hands upon the cross, saying, *"Herein is love, not that we loved God, but that he loved us, and sent His Son to be the propitiation for our sins; and not for ours only, but also for the sins of the whole world."* This is the only truth which can ever triumph effectually over our suspicions of the love of God, or over our aversion to love God. All the hearts ever fully won to Him were won at the cross. The human heart never burns with fervent love to God, nor breaks in real penitence, until it comes to the altar where the heart of the Savior bled and broke as the sacrifice for sin. The loveliness of nature may awaken a momentary admiration of God; and the mighty hand of Providence may sober down the heart into something like softness; and the terrors of judgment awe it into an agitation not unlike repentance; but the genial glow of true love, and the generous meltings of godly sorrow, can only be produced by "Beholding the Lamb of God, as the Lamb slain for us." This was the "great sight" which arrested the attention of the world, when the gospel was first preached. To see this great sight, they turned round from the altars of idolatry, from the oracles of philosophy, from the orgies of superstition, and from the pageants of Greek and Roman festivals: not, indeed, intending, when they turned, to "forsake all and follow," Christ crucified; but only to gratify their curiosity, or, perhaps, to find fault with the new religion, at first. They did, however, turn to behold the Lamb of God in the mirror of the gospel; and "being turned," they saw such an express image of God in His character; such proofs of the love of God in His cross, such pledges of the grace of God in His promises, and such a manifestation of the evil of sin and the value of the soul in all the history of the Savior, that they could not, for a time, withdraw their eyes from the Apocalypse of mercy. Thousands wondered, wept, and were won, at the first glance; and never again looked back to the altars of Jupiter or Venus, Mars or Diana: and even those who turned their backs on the cross, were never again able to look at their altars with confidence. Thus the love of many was won to the true God, and the false gods lost both the love and the respect of those who continued to worship them.

Why is not the cross thus heart-conquering still? Why has it not gained the confidence of your soul, and thus the love of your heart? It is easy to say, in answer to this question, that the Holy Spirit has not "directed your heart unto the love of God," by the attractions of the cross of Christ. For, why has He not? When did you ask Him to do so?

When did you give Him any opportunity of doing so? Have you ever placed yourself under the cross for "one hour," to look on the Lamb of God, as "slain" for your sins, and as "pierced" by your sins? If not—why not?

You have read, thought, wept, over other histories of suffering. Our patriots, philanthropists, and martyrs have arrested your notice; and you would reckon yourself unmanly did you not admire their heroism, and sympathize with their fate. But could you have felt thus for them and with them, had you read or thought of them, no more than you have contemplated the character and sacrifice of the Savior! Why then, should the Spirit work whilst you are idle? What has He to work upon in your mind? He works by means: and the means of grace are not all tried, when you visit the sanctuary on the Sabbath.

Public means are both preparation and obligation for private study and prayer. Indeed, their first great object is to make men thoughtful and prayerful: if, therefore, you resist the Holy Spirit, when He directs you to your Bible and your closet at home, how can you expect Him to shed abroad the love of God in your heart? Do consider how you place yourself by this neglect. When—where—could the Spirit of God find you at leisure, or so unoccupied with other things, that He could have a fair opportunity of applying the gospel to your heart? You are not ill-engaged now—if you are weighing these appeals. Well; will you make the most of this moment— and close the book—and open your Bible—and fall down before God; and plead, that "now," may be "the accepted time" for love from God, and for love to God?

Have you done so? If not—why not? Both the love of His heart, and a heart to love Him, are worth asking for—and you would pray for them, with strong cries and tears, were you sure that "this night your soul would be required of you." Is not this true? You cannot bear to think of entering eternity uninterested in the love of God. How then can you retire to rest, or to business, without prayer for this infinite blessing? You would not sleep less calmly, after fervent prayer for grace of the Holy Spirit. And, what business would be interrupted or embarrassed by the cheering and inspiring consciousness that you had entreated the love of the God of love, and tendered to Him the affectionate homage of your soul? You might thus retire from the mercy-seat to your pillow to be fanned asleep as by the wings of its watching cherubim; or to your sphere of labor as if led by a guiding star of its shekinah.

2

Of Manly Impartiality in Repentance

That the morning stars should have sang together, and all the angelic "sons of God shouted for joy" both when the top stone of creation was brought forth, and when the Mediator of Redemption was born, does not surprise us: the events were worthy of the golden harps of all the celestial Hierarchy; for Creation and Redemption were made for each other, and both the work of Christ: but that "joy" should circulate thus widely and warmly amongst "the angels of God in heaven," when "one sinner repenteth," is as surprising as it is pleasing. It is however as true as that all the angels of God worshipped the Savior at His birth. He who received this homage from them on earth, and to whom all their harps are tributary in heaven, bore this testimony to their general and generous delight in the repentance of sinners.

The repentance of a sinner is not, however, just that point in his history at which we should expect this "joy" to begin: for, to all penitential feeling, all the angels of God are personally utter strangers. They are all indeed much humbler before the throne than the humblest penitent now at the footstool: but then humility is unmixed with shame or sorrow, and uninfluenced by any contrasts, except those which finite perfection will forever present to infinite perfection, and finite gratitude to infinite goodness. They never sinned, and therefore, they can no more sorrow than they can suffer. Such being the facts of their moral and mental constitution, we might suppose, reasoning from it, that their joy over a sinner would not begin until he had made some considerable progress in holiness: or at least not until his own joy began. We could not expect, had we not been told, that angels would take up their harps to celebrate his conversion before he himself took down his harp from the willows. They do not, however, suspend their song until he can sing too. Their joy begins with his godly sorrow; their triumph with his tears; their congratulations with his sighs. The moment he smites on his breast, saying, *"God be merciful unto me a sinner,"* they strike their harps, singing, *"Salvation, and glory, and honor, unto God the Lamb."*

This is, indeed, great attention to penitents. It is, however, the least of all the attentions which Repentance on earth obtains in heaven: for *"the High and Lofty One, who inhabiteth eternity, Whose name is Holy, saith,' I dwell with him that is of a contrite and humble spirit, to revive the spirit of the humble, and to revive the heart of the contrite ones.'"* Thus also saith Jehovah, *"Heaven is My throne, and the earth is my footstool; and to this man will I look; even to him that is poor, and of a contrite spirit, and trembleth at my word."* This look of love and pity from the eye of Omniscience eclipses all angelic sympathy: this paternal joy of Jehovah, when a lost son is found again, both eclipses and explains all the joy of angels over a penitent. Their smiles are but the reflection of the light of His countenance; and their songs but the echo of His welcome to returning prodigals. And as this accounts for all that angels feel and do on behalf of the penitent, so this paternal joy of the Father has its explanation in the blood of the Lamb which ransomed, and in the grace of the Spirit which regenerated the lost sinner. Thus, all heaven thrills with lively interest and delight, whenever a human heart thrills with "godly sorrow."

"With joy the Father doth approve
The fruit of His eternal love.
The Son, with joy, looks down and sees

The purchase of his agonies.
The Spirit takes delight to view
The holy soul he formed anew,
And saints and angels join to sing
The growing empire of their king."

Now, must there not be, on earth, something unfavorable to repentance, seeing repentance is thus taken under such special and splendid patronage in heaven? What, then, is that hindrance, in the world and in the heart, to counteract which all heaven is thus wonderfully in array? God does nothing unnecessary in kind nor degree. There is no parade in His arrangements, and no pretense in His words. He never dignifies what is little, nor gives undue importance to any creature or thing in the universe. There must, therefore, be something in repentance itself that justifies this amazing concentration of angelic and divine sympathies upon it; and something in the world which renders such a patronage of repentance necessary; for, upon no other point of a Christian's history, and on no other part of his religious character, is the attention of Heaven thus signally drawn. Neither his faith nor his love, his patience or his zeal, is represented as sending sensations of visible joy through all the heaven of heavens. Not, however, that these graces of the Spirit are inferior to repentance: there is a sense in which both faith and love are superior to it: and, accordingly, they are honored above it, although in another way. Hence more promises are made to faith, than to repentance. It is to faith, not to repentance, that eternal life is pledged. It is by faith, not by repentance, that pardon and justification are obtained. Still, it is the revealed fact, that repentance first engages the public attention of heaven. The harps and hymns of glory are vocal around it; and the whole pavilion of eternity reverberates with the welcome which sounds from the throne, when a trembling sinner is contrite. This is as wisely, as it is wonderfully, arranged.

Repentance is thus publicly and signally honored in heaven, because it is generally despised on earth, and naturally disliked by the human heart. God has, therefore, vouchsafed to throw the whole weight of His own complacency, and all the force of angelic opinion, into the scale, against the scorn of the world and the pride of the heart. He knows how both the laugh and the frown of the multitude can sway the individual; and, therefore, upon the "contrite ones," or one by one, and even on "one sinner that repenteth," He brings all the smiles of heaven to bear at once. This is as considerate as it is condescending. Alas!—however, that it should be necessary. It is indeed surprising and pleasing; but it places both us and the world in a sad light. It tells a melancholy tale.

Repentance should not require the shield or the enshrinements of heaven to protect it. Bare permission to repent ought to be welcomed with acclamation in a world where all have sinned and come short of the glory of God. Time and place for repentance should be enough to secure it in all, seeing that without it the best must perish. Besides, we do repent, and that too almost instinctively and spontaneously when we offend a benefactor or a friend whom we love. We are not easy in our own mind until we have done something to heal the wound given to his mind. We do not require him to implore us to be reconciled unto him again: much less do we render it necessary that he should double all his former kindness before we are willing to confess our faults. This is as it should be; and thus we do feel and act when our happiness or success in life depends upon an injured friend.

Now, our happiness and success in both worlds depend entirely and eternally on God. Without His providence, we cannot enjoy the life that now is; nor without His grace, inherit the life which is to come. But, how can we expect either, if we are unwilling to repent? We risk both whilst we allow impenitence. It can only "treasure up wrath against the day of wrath;" and as that day will be "the revelation of the righteous judgment of God," we, and all men, might well rush to repentance at once, and in a body, even if the call to repent were pealed only by the trumpets and thunders of the judgment-seat. It is not, however, by terrors chiefly, that God urges repentance. He speaks indeed from the depths and darkness of the eternity He inhabits, even when He consoles "the contrite ones:" but this is not done to terrify or intimidate them; but to arrest their notice to His condescension, and to assure them of His perfect sincerity. God's invite invokes, woos us to repent, as if His own paternal happiness hinged upon our penitential spirit. And, lest words of solicitude and welcome should be misunderstood, He puts forward all His angels, not with trumpets of authority, nor with vials of judgment, but as it were with harps of jubilee that thus they may be living illustrations of His own joy, and satisfactory interpreters of His good will towards man.

It can hardly fail to occur to you now that it is not every mood nor emotion of sorrow for sin, which amounts to that repentance which thus delights God and gives joy to the angels of God. All that obtains the name of repentance on earth is not likely to be held reality in heaven. Angels are too wise to be rash, and too holy to be partial, in judging of penitence. For, however they acquire their knowledge of any "one sinner that repenteth," that knowledge becomes "joy in the presence of God" to them: and this, it would not be allowed to become, if the repentance were insincere or equivocal. You feel at once, that neither the trembling of Felix, nor the remorse of Judas, could mislead the angels of God. The halter of the traitor, and the habits of the king, settle the question of their repentance, even to us. Had angels therefore nothing more to guide their judgment, and thus to regulate their joy, but their own high opportunities of observation, and their own native powers of discrimination, they would be in no great danger of mistaking remorse for repentance. And as neither their own powers as spirits, nor their opportunities as "ministering spirits," account fully for the extent of their knowledge, or for the height of their joy, the probability is that their information comes to them direct from the Eternal Throne. God "looks" to the repenting sinner before they discover him; and their eye follows His; and thus they know where to find him, and when to rejoice over him. Father, Son, and Spirit, have acknowledged his penitence before angels minister to his wants, or sympathize with his godly sorrow. Their joy is not, therefore, premature nor precarious. Time will neither refute its warrant, nor reprove its warmth. They now know as well whom to rejoice over in the "day of power," as they will know the wheat from the tares in the day of judgment. Their harps can no more err now than their hands can err then. Men may delude themselves, and deceive others, by apparent repentance; but appearances cannot impose upon angels; because they take the signal for joy from the paternal looks of the Father, from the public intercession of the Son, and from the positive work of the Holy Spirit. Let us not, therefore, impose upon ourselves in this matter.

A superficial repentance cannot be the occasion of angelic joy. The passing pang of regret, and the extorted tear of remorse, and the piercing shriek of death-bed terror, may have no penitence in them; for as old Bishop Hall says, "although a sincere repentance is never too late, a late repentance is seldom sincere." "Were weeping repentance," says Jeremy Taylor, "Hell would be full of penitents; for there is both weeping and gnashing of teeth." Besides, it is not without wise and weighty reasons that God teaches us to bring our repentance to the test of angelic joy. Their joy is impartial judgment; and although we cannot, of course, hear the verdict of angels in our own case, or in that of others, we can form our opinion from what we know of it and them, how our repentance would be likely to approve itself to their judgment, if it were submitted to them. They certainly form an unpacked and impartial jury. They have indeed no kindred feelings with sinners; no "like passions with ourselves:" but then they have no prejudices against us, nor any indifference to our welfare. This is more than could be affirmed, perhaps, of any jury of our fellow-creatures.

When I empanel, in thought, even a circle of my personal friends, and realize the act of submitting any penitence to their judgment, I do not feel quite sure that they would do me full justice, whichever way they decided on my case; and thus I myself cannot judge fairly of it whilst I am only confronted with men: but the moment I confront myself with angels, and ask—is it likely that the kind and degree of sorrow for sin, which I have felt and cultivated, would commend itself to them as cause for joy on my account? I see at once the real character of my own repentance, and can anticipate the verdict I cannot hear.

This is most likely one of the great moral reasons for that heavenly arrangement by which angels are so prominently connected with human repentance. God is indeed the final judge of its sincerity and its impartiality; and we are not wise nor prudent if we do not go all the length of submitting the whole question of our personal repentance to Him, as the searcher of hearts and the discerner of spirits. We are not in good earnest about our penitence until we test it at the Eternal Mind, by considering what God is likely to think of it. We may therefore be quite sure that it is not to divert us from self-examination in His own realized presence that we are allowed and led to realize the probabilities of an angelic verdict in our favor. This intermediate tribunal must be intended, therefore, to pave our way, and help our weakness, in carrying up our appeal to the throne of God. That is solemn work, whether we feel it to be so or not.

Those who are afraid to appeal to the Omniscient for the genuineness of their repentance, cannot but see, however, that this intermediate test of sincerity softens the application of the final test, without lessening its solemnity. I mean, that, in the same way as the expressed favorable opinion of judicious Christian friends helps a timid penitent to open his heart to God for inspection and pity; so the consciousness that even holy angels could hardly doubt his sincerity, whatever they thought of him in other respects, is calculated to help forward his humble appeals and applications to the heart-searching God.

The truth of our repentance is such a solemn question that we may well be glad of any hint which can help us to settle it. Now, although angels cannot give us any personal help, nor may we make any appeal to them even if they could both hear and help us; (which they cannot) still, we can and may try ourselves, by asking, would a good angel think me impenitent; reckon me a hypocrite; deem me but half-hearted? Now if I feel that I should shrink from his scrutiny, and fear his verdict, I have learned by this supposition more of the secrets of my own heart, and am thrown with awful solicitude on the more solemn consideration, that if both my own heart and an angel's opinion condemn me, "God is greater" than both, "and knoweth all things " If again, on the other hand, I can see how a good angel would hardly feel himself at liberty to discredit, or to despise, or to doubt my repentance, I have thus also gained some clearer insight into the frame of my own spirit; and, without being at all elated by discovering some symptoms of a contrite spirit in myself, I am thus encouraged to lay them before God, as the first-fruits of His own Spirit, and to plead more fervently for their increase and maturity.

Thus it is no fanciful speculation I have drawn you into, although there be fancy in it. I want you to think about repentance; and, therefore, I throw you out of the ruts of familiarized phraseology, that you may be compelled to think for yourself in a matter where you must act for yourself, or perish. Dwell therefore on the idea—and let it haunt you—that if you could not make out to the satisfaction of saints or angels a case of real penitence on your own part, how can you approve your sincerity to the God of angels, to the Father of spirits, who searcheth the heart and trieth the reins of the children of men?

But, perhaps you have never yet looked at the subject of repentance in any other light than that in which ordinary opinion places it—as something very proper and necessary in the case of all, before they die; and especially so in the case of those who have been very wild. Now, if this be your view of it, I need hardly tell you that you have not yet deemed it necessary to apply it to yourself. I mean— you do not reckon yourself so very wicked, nor so very near your end, as to require immediate repentance. Accordingly, you have not tried to be truly penitent yet. You cannot, therefore, tell exactly how your heart or conscience would feel, were you to set yourself to try the duty, just at present. It, is however, well worth your while, to ask yourself even now, "what would I do, were I to set about my repentance tonight?" Well; what would you do? How would you begin? You intend to make the attempt, in the course of your life, and not to leave the duty to the hazards of a death-bed. This is wise. But, if you do not see now how to proceed; if you feel at a loss how to act; if you cannot help feeling that repentance would be awkward work, even at this moment of health and composure—it is only wise to ask what likelihood is there that you could make more of it at any future period of your life? You surely do not wish that some startling calamity should befall you, to give a penitential turn to your thoughts and feelings. And yet if you are conscious that you could make little or nothing of repentance at present, were you to try the duty tonight—what certainty or probability is there that you would be better prepared for the attempt, some years hence? True; you expect to be wiser as you grow older. Shall I, then, accept this apology from you? No; look at it before you offer it again: it is an actual confession that you are now so foolish as not to know how to proceed, if you had to repent or perish this night!

"But," you will say, "the Holy Spirit convinces of sin, and thus leads to repentance; and I do hope that He will work thus upon my mind, and give me grace to repent truly, and in good time." This is really making bad, worse, if you really mean what you say, and have not yet begun to pray earnestly and habitually for the grace of the Holy Spirit. He is, indeed, the only Author of repentance unto life, and without his quickening influences no man can repent: but it is just as true that no man who is unwilling to repent now has any right or warrant to hope that the Holy Spirit will step in, some years hence, to make him willing, by a "day of power."

God's "days of power," are not provided for the purpose of prolonging our days of impenitence and delay: and no man has less reason to expect such a day in his own case, than you who know that it is absolutely necessary, and yet have not begun to pray fervently for it. There is meanness, as well as presumption, in such conduct.

Do look well at the position you have placed yourself in. The best that can be said of your case is—that you have not lost sight of the necessity of personal repentance: nor made up your mind to postpone it to your last moments: nor cut with all the means by which grace is communicated. Thus, you have not ventured to go "altogether out of the way," in which the Holy Spirit meets with sinners, to make them penitent. You read something on the subject of eternal salvation, and hear more, and occasionally give some time to both meditation and prayer.—You could not be satisfied if you neglected these things entirely. You know and believe too much about your soul to abandon it recklessly and rashly to mere chance. But, are you not risking it upon a very bare and slight probability, whilst neither your prayers nor meditations take a penitential form? Now, this, they have not done yet: and this they cannot do whilst they only wander around the general subject of religion, and but just keep within sight of the fatal consequences of irreligion. Such "far off," and vague glances at all the claims of piety, will never bring you to the point with any one of its claims. You must go fully up to and fairly meet some one of them, to begin with, if you would have the whole of them brought to bear upon your character, eventually or ever: for this vague glancing at all things in religion, without grappling with anything, leads to nothing that is either saving or satisfactory. How could it?

Piety is both a personal and progressive thing; and must, therefore, begin with some definite object, and distinct purpose. And what is so proper to begin at as repentance? Without repentance nothing else will go on well, nor end in salvation. Unrepented sin will not be pardoned. Unrepented folly will not be forgiven. Unrepented indecision and delay will not obtain mercy, however mercy may be asked. Indeed, there will be no asking—that amounts to praying for mercy to pardon, or grace to help, until the evil of sin and the guilt of shortcoming are seriously laid to heart. Words, however appropriate or emphatic, are neither confession nor prayer. The heart must feel the guilt of sin, and thirst for the hope of pardon, before the words of the lips can become confession or supplication.

Do not, therefore, try everything at once, if you would do anything well. This has been your great error hitherto. You have thought a little about sin—and a little about duty—and a little about grace—and a little about salvation—and a little about eternity; but not enough about any one of them, to bring you fully to the point in religion. In this way also you have prayed : with some reference to your sins—and some to your weakness—and some to your temptations—and some to your difficulties—and some to your final safety; but without any concentration of prayer upon the turning point in personal religion. This will not do. You must have a definite object, if you would be a decided Christian. It is indeed all very well, so far, that both your thoughts and prayers have taken "a bird's-eye view" of the whole matter. Everything you know and feel, on the general subject of piety, may be turned to good account, at any given point of piety. All the lines of your meditations and emotions may meet in any one duty of religion—and in none, with more advantage, than in repentance; because all that you have thought, and felt, and tried in religion will furnish reasons for penitence.

You now see how matters stand between yourself and God. They are not, indeed, in the worst state that things could be in; but they are in a very unsettled state. They are anything but hopeless; and not at all unpromising; but still, they are equivocal. In the emphatic language of Him who searcheth the heart, *"you are neither hot nor cold."* Thus, it is what you call your religion, or what you consider to be the best symptoms of some piety—quite as much as what you reckon to be your sins—that makes repentance your immediate duty. For, were there even less guilt on your conscience than you must confess to be—and thus less reason for alarm because of actual sins—the state of your heart before God—so divided—so vacillating—so temporizing—is itself enough to startle you.

Indeed, if your consciousness of personal guilt awakens but little fear, and less sorrow, I doubt very much whether you will ever become a penitent at all, except you begin by repenting of what you have taken up with as your personal religion. This is no paradox, however much it may surprise you at first. You have quite as much cause to be alarmed at your kind and degree of piety as at your actual sins. I do not mean, of course, that you can or ought to repent of any attention you have paid to religion; nor of any restraint you have laid on your passions; nor of any good habit you have adhered to: but I do mean—that nothing perils your soul more than your partial and superficial regard to religion. That both beguiles and blinds you. It is just enough to distinguish you from such as "care for none of these things;" but not enough to decide your choice or your character. How could it!

You balance what is bad about you by what is good: not, perhaps, for the purpose of making the good a meritorious set off against the demerit of the bad: you may be quite above that vulgar legality; but you do set off the good, as an excuse for not repenting of the bad immediately; and thus allow the former to hush up or prevent the fears which the latter should awaken.

Meet your own case now fairly. You can look back upon the tenor of your life without much shame; and even on your sins without much compunction or fear. You cannot call any regrets you feel true repentance. You do not think yourself a real penitent yet. You admit all this. Well; just ask yourself now, "What is there to melt or touch my heart, if my past sins and short-comings fail to do so? I certainly do not intend to commit greater sins, in order to arrive at the proper sense of the evil of sin. That would be more likely to sear my heart and conscience, than to soften them. How then am I to become a penitent? The past does not alarm or humble me deeply; and I do not wish with the future to furnish greater occasion for repentance."

Does this bring you to the point? If so—look into what is comparatively good about you, and you will find in it abundant cause for both shame and grief. You cannot take a full view of the bright side of your character without being shocked: for beneath what is best and fairest, there lurk motives, desires, feelings, and thoughts, which will hardly bear naming or analyzing. Your general reverence for the majesty and authority of God (for you have not loved Him yet) is perhaps as creditable to your understanding as anything which distinguishes you from the ungodly. You could not take profane or vulgar liberties with His holy name. You would not dare His wrath nor arraign His justice.

But you—even you—have almost wished that God were more lenient to sin, and less severe in punishing it; and this you have wished—on your own account, and for your own sinful or slothful purposes. Is not this cause for immediate repentance? Can you think of what you have wished God both to be and to do, without hiding your face?

Again; your general veneration for the Holy Scriptures is highly creditable to your judgment and taste. You see upon their surface, and feel in their spirit, that they are the lively oracles of the living God. You would not join nor countenance an attack upon their authority. And yet, you have not often listened to these oracles as the voice of God: there are books you are fonder of than the Bible: there are some parts of it you do not like, and others that you do not willingly believe: and, although you feel incapable of jesting with it as a whole, you have ventured to utter or contemplate a jest upon certain points of Scripture. I am not making out an extreme case against you, in this matter. I leave it to your own conscience to fill up what is wanting in this charge. And, can you remember that the word of the living, true, and eternal God, has been little read, less studied, and still less prayed over, and yet be unmoved or un-melted? You have not, indeed, treated it worse than others, nor so ill as many; but you—even you—have trifled with His holy oracles.

Take up your Bible, and let it tell the history of its treatment at your hands, since the day that your parents' hands (now perhaps closed in death, or clasped in prayer for you) put it into them. And now —surely, you could shed a tear on that little-used, and less improved gift. If not— you have less heart and conscience too, than I wished to give you credit for. It is high time, indeed, for you to concentrate all your prayers in the cry— "Take away the heart of stone."

Again; you have taken some steadfast looks at both the requirements of Eternity. You are not unacquainted with, nor indifferent to the glories of heaven, or the end of sin and sinners in hell. Your thoughts have ascended at times, like an eagle, amongst the sublime or the sweet realities of paradise, until you have—

*"Wished for wings to fly away,
To bask in its eternal day;"*

and they have descended, like a stone cast into the lake of fire, until you were resolved to flee from the wrath to come. But you have neither fled from that wrath—nor laid hold on eternal life. You have not lost sight of either; but you have left the question—"which must be my portion?"—unsettled. This is cause for both shame and sorrow.

You are not ignorant, nor insensible; and yet you are undecided in the face of realizing glimpses of heaven and hell, any one of which ought to be more influential than a flaming sword, to stop your procrastination. Do look at your heart! It is eternal things with which it thus plays fast and loose. It is eternal worlds, which it allows this world to dim and displace. It is all the love of God can give, and all the wrath of God can do, which it trifles with. You surely cannot think of this—without seeing, and feeling too, your immediate need of "a new heart and a right spirit." This is, however, not all, nor the worst. Perhaps the very best feature of your case is that both the character and the cross of the Savior are not uninteresting to you. You have no sympathy with minds which can see no beauty in the person of Immanuel, or no sublimity in His atonement. You cannot deem him less than God in our nature, nor reckon his sacrifice less than a propitiation for our sins. You are, indeed, aware of the mysteries you admit, in thus adoring His godhead, and admiring His mediation: but you are aware also, that all this is done in the heaven of heavens, where neither angels nor saints can err; and that nothing else can be made out from the Bible, without a process of refusing and refining its testimony, incompatible with all the claims of a revelation from God. Now, none of your religious sentiments is more creditable in you than this one. In no judgment of your own mind, do you come so near to the first principles of glorified minds. It is in harmony with all the creed and chorus of heaven. And yet—here it is that you are chiefly guilty before God, and most need repentance: for you have trifled with this Divine —this atoning Savior! You have not fully and finally committed your soul to Him, although you know that His soul was made an offering for sin—that His blood cleanseth from all sin—that His love passeth knowledge, and that the riches of His grace are unsearchable.

Here is guilt, before which the crimson of ordinary crimes become pale! Here is treachery of heart, before which the scarlet of practical compromise becomes faint. I am not exaggerating nor declaiming. You yourself admit your need of a Divine and Atoning Savior: you accord this rank to the slain Lamb of God:—and yet, you have not fled to his cross for refuge; but only stood afar off, looking at it as a refuge, you intend to seek, at some future period. Is not this, to take unhallowed and daring liberties with the dying love of Christ—is not this base ingratitude? Does not this touch your heart, and make tears blind your eyes, and so "loosen the joints of your knees," that you must fall down at the foot of the cross as a penitent? Oh, it is in what has been your religion that you must look for reasons for immediate repentance, if you can look un-melted upon your other sins. Your heart has evinced its alienation and depravity, in common with all hearts, although not in the same way. It has tampered and trifled with grace, even whilst paying some homage to law. It has put forward a partial subjection to the scepter of the Savior, as an apology for delaying a personal submission to His cross.

I will not ask now, if it be unmanly to give way to shame and sorrow before God? All the unmanliness has been in standing out so long against the godlike claims of the great salvation. Angels, who need not that salvation, have been far more affected by it then you: aye, and have felt more holy impatience for your repentance than you have cherished. Years ago, they would have hailed it with joy: and even now, it will fill them with joy. And, surely, if they are not ashamed to rejoice over you, you need not be ashamed to avow yourself a penitent before men, any more than before God. For, if it be not un-angelic to honor penitence, it cannot be unmanly to avow it.

If, therefore, you are now determined to "give yourself unto the Lord," determine also to "give yourself to the church, according to the will of God." Let it be felt also in the world that you are not ashamed to "confess" a Savior who has promised to "confess you before his Father and all his angels." Then, the harps that hymned your repentance with joy, will hymn with rapture, your acquittal at the judgment-seat, and your ascent to heaven.

If you be, now, concerned to "sorrow after a godly sort," do propose to yourself, and set yourself to pursue nothing less than to please God by the penitence of your spirit. This is a rule in all duty so useful and essential, and yet so little used or studied, that I cannot but refer you to my own little work on "Pleasing God; a Guide to the Conscientious." I would not thus violate modesty, by commending anything of my own to your notice, if I knew of any other book founded upon the principle of pleasing God in repenting and believing.

3

Of Manly Avowals of Immortal Hopes

Until "the hope of glory" acquire such an ascendency in the modern as it had in the primitive church, no great impression will be made upon the world. Nothing but this "good hope through grace," can arrest general attention, or conciliate prejudice. The holiness of the church however beautiful, and her harmony however perfect, would have but little influence apart from the prevalence of a hope full of everlasting life. It is, indeed, equally true, that no public manifestation of hope, however tranquil or triumphant, would gain respect in the world, apart from corresponding holiness and peace. The world both expects and demands consistency from the avowed followers of Christ. Not, however, that the world loves holiness, or admires harmony for their own sake, nor because of their moral bearings on the glory of God: but because inconsistencies and controversies in the church furnish convenient weapons of assault or defense against the claims of religion. This is the real secret of the world's attention to the personal consistency of communicants, and to the relative spirit of churches. The falls of professors and the strife of churches are watched and pilloried not because God is dishonored, nor because religion is discredited by them; but because they can be played off as excuses for not making any profession of religion at all. Were, therefore, the church of Christ all in character and spirit that the world says she ought to be; and, in addition to this, all that God says she ought to be: "a glorious church, without spot or wrinkle," the world would drop the mask it now wears, and gnash its teeth against such a display of holiness. For it cares nothing about the want of holiness in the church, except so far as that want may affect the business of life, and furnish pretenses for the neglect of godliness.

Were it possible therefore for the church to become, like her apocalyptic representative, "clothed with the sun" of purity, and encircled with the rainbow of peace, apart from "abounding in hope," she could not win the world. No degree of worth of character on her side would weigh effectually on the other side, without the prevalence of more and better hopes of eternal glory, than she now avows or cherishes. Her hopes must strike the world before the world will copy her holiness. Yea; she herself must be more struck with her eternal prospects before she can grow much in purity or peace. Her holiness is low, because her hope is languid. A glance at the history of the primitive churches will both illustrate and justify these hints. I want you therefore to seek at the mercy-seat, and to accept at the cross, such lively hopes of eternal happiness as cannot be concealed from your friends or foes, nor remain doubtful or uninspiring to yourself. Such a good hope may be obtained and maintained "through grace." It may beam in the eye, and breathe on the lips, and give its own character to your life, as well as any other pleasing hope. And it certainly is not a hope to be ashamed of. It will bear comparison with any and all the hopes which brighten or sweeten life. It will stand the test of all the principles, which justify the love of the avowal of earthly hopes.

You are not ashamed to cherish or manifest before your companions the hope of success in business; nor the hope of domestic happiness; nor the hope of intellectual enjoyment; nor the hope of some eventual proficiency in your favorite line of study. You are right. You have no occasion to be ashamed of any rational hope, or laudable pursuit. Hopeless labor is always heartless labor, and generally unsuccessful. Why not then hope openly; hope ardently, hope habitually, for eternal life? That is not without the charms or the charities of social enjoyment: for it is everlasting fellowship with all the unfallen and restore intelligence of the universe. That is not without the pleasures of knowledge, or the expansion of mind: for it is access to all the arcana of nature, and to all the archives of time and eternity, with leisure to ransack and ability to comprehend, them all. That is not without the calm joys of home, or the spirit-stirring ecstasies of great events: for it is alternately the retirement of a mansion in heaven, or the splendor of special audiences in the heaven of heavens. That is not without safety or solace: it is the eternal absence of all risk or change, and the eternal presence of all security and satisfaction; for it is at the right hand of God and the Lamb, and there the joy is full and the pleasure is forever more. Thus the hope of domestic happiness is not perfect apart from an eternity of it in heaven. The hope of mental improvement is not perfect, apart from an eternity of it in heaven. The hope of personal enjoyment is not perfect, apart from "everlasting consolation." And all this is included in "good hope through grace."

Christ in the heart is the hope of all the glory which God can give or eternity prolong. And, why should not all this hope be embraced and cherished? It is not more than is warranted by the promise of God. The rest they look for will arise from the enlargement of their knowledge, as well as from the cessation of their cares: the rapture they anticipate will all center in the Savior, because He is the source of all its sources, and the center of all its centers: but it will spring from all the worlds of His empire, and from all the wonders of his providence, as well as from His presence and glory. There is, therefore, no harm, no sentimentalism, no refining upon sober and solemn facts, in realizations of heaven which include more than adoring gratitude for redemption, and more than "joy unspeakable" for perfect freedom from all sin. For in the fullness of joy, which constitutes that unspeakable glory, there is the joy of perfect knowledge; the joy of high and holy friendship; the joy of expanding intellect and exploring study, under the light of eternity, and in the company of all its first-born spirits. It is, remember —a word—a country—a kingdom—a city—as well as a temple—that is held up to us in the heaven of the Bible. It opens upon us, radiant in all that can entrance our powers of contemplation, and rich in all that can employ our powers of action. It has work for us as men, as well as worship for us as redeemed sinners. It is prepared for our rational nature, as well as for our regenerated spirit; for our social sympathies, as well as for our fellowship with God.

Now, although I am persuaded of the fact, and feelingly alive to the principle, that no man ever did or can lay hold of the hope of eternal life for the sake of what is intellectual, or for the sake of what is social, or for the sake of what is sublime in its immortal joys; I cannot, and will not, shut my eyes to the fact that these things, as well as the new song, and in common with all the holiness and hallelujahs of the New Jerusalem, are component parts of the happiness of heaven; and ought, therefore, to have their natural influence upon our minds. No man, indeed, will, even for the sake of eternal fellowship with the innumerable company of angels; nor for the sake of sitting down with the noble army of martyrs; nor for the sake of unveiling Nature through all her works, and Providence through all its mysteries, and Glory through all its shrines, ever consent or desire to be a penitent at the cross, or a suppliant at the mercy-seat, or a pilgrim in the world, or a pillar in the church, or a sufferer in the furnace. Alas, no man ceases to be manly, mind to be mental, and spirit to be aspiring, when they are brought into contact with the "glory, honor, and immortality, of eternal life." The great become groveling, and the noble mean, and the enterprising driveling, when they are wooed by celestial distinctions. Any crown but a crown of glory will be run for, in our world. Nothing in heaven, notwithstanding all that is in it, melts or moves any man effectually, until the safety it provides for his soul, touches his heart. Until then, we care nothing for its thrones, crowns, palms, or harps. They appeal to us in vain, until we become afraid of perishing. In one sense, I am not at all sorry for this: for, did heavenly and eternal distinctions commend themselves to the pride, the ambition, or the envy of the human heart, just as earthly distinctions lay hold upon its passions, heaven would tend, as much as the earth, to divert the mind from the Savior and the Sanctifier. Its glories, if they captivated as distinctions at first, would counteract the designs of grace.

It is, therefore, wisely ordered, that we can make nothing satisfactory or inspiring of future glory, until we feel our need of grace. No soul desires heaven until it dreads hell. No soul thinks of coming to Christ for anything that is in heaven until it begins to come to Him for the pardon of sin, and thus for deliverance from the wrath to come. All the bright hopes of immortality unfold from the humble hopes of pardon and acceptance. It is only when we go as lost, to Him who lives to seek, and who died to save the lost, that we see or feel the worth and weight of glory. In a word; we do not look at eternal life seriously until we form the habit of "looking for the mercy of the Lord Jesus Christ, unto eternal life."

Nothing, therefore, is farther from my intention than to fascinate you with visions of intellectual or social enjoyments in heaven of which the Lamb slain is not the source and center. He is "all in all," in all the glory of the scenes and the society above. Just because He is so, however, I would lead out your hopes to all that glory, that you may see in the full blaze of its light, the worth, the capacity, and the demerits of your soul; and thus learn at once your need of a Savior, and the all-sufficiency of Christ to save you. Just because I am sure that you will not stir one step to secure the crown until you betake yourself to the cross for escape from the curse, I show you all the crown, as well as all the curse, and combine the attractions of the former with the terrors of the latter, to hasten your flight to the cross for personal safety. Let, then, safety be your first object: but let it not be your only nor your chief aim. It is, indeed, much; but it is not all that is provided and promised by the gospel. It is the basis on which all the eternal weight of glory must rest and be raised, whatever be the eventual weight or height of that glory; but, still, it is only the basis, and not at all the "building," which God has prepared for them that love him.

The first Christians knew and believed this fact; and, therefore, their hopes laid hold upon all the glory that is "laid up in heaven:" upon its honors, as well as its ease; upon its raptures as well as its rest; upon its intellectual light as well as upon its moral loveliness. They hoped to "reign as kings and priests" with the Savior, as well as to be with him beholding his glory; and just because both felicities were equally promised by Christ. Nor was this all: the wide and firm hold they thus took upon the inheritance of the saints in light enabled them to take a corresponding hold upon the inheritance of the saints in the wilderness. I mean, that such were their enlarged and lively hopes of future happiness in heaven that their hopes of present guidance and guardianship on earth were firm and bright. They calculated on such a weight of glory above and forever that they found it easy to expect a sufficiency of grace below, and as long as they needed grace to help. Thus their joy became not only "unspeakable," because it was "full of glory;" but, for the same reason it was practical, compensating and sustaining, under all the trials of life and godliness. This was the good effect of their good hope upon themselves. And now, I want you to mark minutely, the reaction of their hope upon the world: for its influence did not terminate in their own happiness; but that happiness so attracted the notice of others, as to excite general curiosity about the "reason" of the hope that produced it. Accordingly, all the primitive Christians were specially taught by the apostles, to expect so much inquiry into the real cause of their hope, that it became one of their chief duties, to be *"ready always to give an answer to every man that asked for a reason of the hope which was in them."* The bare mention of this fact will remind you, that the present aspect of hope amongst Christians in general, is neither so amazing nor commanding as to excite curiosity or compel inquiry after its reasons. Were the hope of eternal life, as it is now held and exhibited by the church, to create a question in the world, that question, alas, must be —what is the reason that there is so little hope; so little heavenly-mindedness; and so much fear of death—amongst those who profess to believe the gospel? The world does not, however, trouble the church with inquiries into the cause of doubts and fears; but is rather pleased, than surprised, to find that they prevail to a very great extent, even amongst the truly pious. Thus, this want of positive enjoyment amongst Christians, like the defects of their character, becomes another convenient weapon for the world, to wield against godliness.

"What do I lose by neglecting religion, if that feeble and fluctuating hope, is all that you have gained, after years of godliness?" said a happy young man to a venerable pilgrim, who was the victim of low spirits. This was not a fair question, when put to an infirm old man; nor can it be fairly put to any Christian at all times. It is, however, a question which those who want excuses will start, when they are hard pressed by their pious friends on the subject of personal religion. And, how few can answer it satisfactorily—by an appeal to the triumphs or the tranquility of their own hope. The time was, however, (and why should it not return) when neither the shrewdest nor the fiercest enemies of Christianity durst ask such a question. The church gave the world other work, and forced upon it the question—how are ye so happy; what is the reason of the hope that is in you?

The history of this period will repay your attention. It is something like this; whilst both the sentiments and character of the first Christians surprised their old companions who continued idolaters, it was their "lively hope," that excited most astonishment. Their religious opinions were felt to be singular, and their godly habits to be strange: but their hopes were utterly unaccountable: they were so many, and all so full of life, and thus so unlike the spirit of the age. That spirit, so far as it was philosophical, was atheistic; and, so far as it was superstitious, its future prospects had no fascinations for the old or the young. The weary eye of age or suffering could not repose on them for solace, nor the eagle-eye of youth turn to them for inspiration. They deserved not and therefore hardly obtained, the name of hopes: so destitute were they of all power to charm or cheer the human mind. Accordingly, the popular, as well as the philosophic maxim was, "Let us eat and drink for to-morrow we die." In such a "region and shadow of death," even Athens and Rome stood. In this dark valley, both the learned and illiterate "sat for ages," looking at each other with despair or scorn. From time to time, someone started up, after profound study, and perambulated the valley, parading a new theory of mind, or matter, or morals; and for a time, the hopeless spectators forgot their misery, in the discussion of mystery. But they discussed only to discard: for as no theory of the universe or of religion brought any cheering hopes home to their bosoms, the people soon fell back upon their old maxim, and sought relief from the cravings of their spirit, in the gratification of their senses.

But when the apostles of the Lamb penetrated into this region and shadow of death, illuminating immortality by the gospel, and throwing "new heavens" over the old earth— their appeal to "what was in man," and to what God had just done for man, by the cross of His Son, and the Sword of His Spirit, could not be disposed of so soon or easily as abstract theories of morals had been. This was "a new thing in the earth." The gospel laid hold upon all the soul's natural "longings" after immortality, and addressed itself to all the points of the soul, at which the heart bled, or the conscience burned, or the understanding craved. This appeal itself was treated, by the generality as a mere theory, too, for a time: but, when here and there, all through the dark valley of heathenism, now a few, and anon many, began to flee from the wrath to come, and to lay hold upon the hope set before them in the gospel, and to avow that hope as their own, and to stand ready to avouch it by their blood; then, even the hopeless and the hardened were absolutely amazed. And when mockery could not move, nor authority silence, nor martyrdom intimidate the converts of the cross, "the world turned upside down" with wonder. It scorned their opinions and hated their principles: but it was staggered by their hopes, in spite of itself; they were so new in their aspect, and so noble in their bearing, and so independent of all the usual motives which had ever influenced the patience, the emulation, or the fortitude of mankind. What was to be done?

Sages pronounced Christianity to be visionary. Senators denounced it as sedition. Priesthood arraigned it as impiety. Crowns rallied armies to crush it. But all in vain. When these forces moved in phalanx against it, they could somewhat hinder it from spreading on the spot where they battled: but even there they could not quench its spirit in the hearts of its votaries nor prevent the heroism of its martyrdom from winning new martyrs. The more the world fought, the more the church conquered: for the children of hope "sung praises unto God" in all their prisons; shouted victory at the stake, and smiled composure at the tribunal. Even women "waxed valiant," beyond the daring of Socrates, and slaves proved that emperors could not shackle spirits which Christ had made free.

Christians of all ranks, recognized only the chariots of God, in the kindling flames; only rivers hastening to the sea of glory, in the engulfing waters: only signals of a summons to heaven, in the flashing sword of persecutors. At length, the state was glad to stay the carnage, that it might save the empire: for headsmen actually wearied of wielding the axe, and soldiers of brandishing the sword, and jailers of riveting chains, and spies of detecting victims, and servants of kindling fires, and judges of signing sentences, and emperors of issuing edicts of extermination: all were wearied out long before the church complained.

A hope that thus defied and defeated the world could not be overlooked. Accordingly, public curiosity began to inquire into its reasons, when imperial vengeance could no longer afford to make war against its votaries. And then Christianity began to triumph gloriously. Every man had been stirred up to ask a reason for the hope it inspired; and every Christian stood ready to give a reason for it; and thus all the church became, virtually, preachers of the gospel. "The Spirit and the Bride," as well as the Spirit and the Ministry, said to the world, "Come and take of the water of life freely." That this is a fair report of the case needs no other proof than the fact that these are the express words of "Jesus Christ, the faithful and true witness." He bowed the heavens, after His ascension, to testify, that the bride said "Come;" and, that the invitation which the church thus gave to the world was, like His own preaching, first and chiefly, a call to lay hold on the hope of eternal life, or to drink of the water of life freely. Thus, there was more than ministerial effort and influence, brought to bear upon the world. Ministers could do more than point to "a River of the water of life, proceeding out of the throne of God and the Lamb, and flowing openly down to the earth: they could point also to thousands, standing all along its banks, who did more than admire it—more than compliment it—more than wish to drink of it—yea, more than hope to drink of it: they had drank so abundantly of its living waters that they could not thirst again for sinful enjoyments, nor cease to long to drink of this river at its fountain head in heaven.

Thus there came from all the churches both a loud echo to the ministerial invitations of the gospel, and a living exemplification of the immediate and immortal advantages of complying with them. And neither the echo nor the example was overlooked by the world. The Corinthian Christians were an "Epistle, known and read of all men." The faith of the Romans was "spoken of throughout the whole world." And the word of the Lord, so "sounded out" from the Thessalonians, that their "God-ward" and heavenward faith was "spread abroad everywhere;" and so spoke for itself, that Paul said, "we need not to speak anything."

This was the aspect and spirit of Christian hope, then, upon the earthly banks of the river of life. That aspect was solemn, but not sad: that spirit "meek" but not timid. Hope embraced such an "exceeding weight" of eternal glory, that it could neither be flippant nor cowardly; silent nor talkative; ostentatious nor shrinking; obtrusive nor ashamed. No; it partook largely of both the solemnity and the loveliness of the immortality, of which it was so full; and, as it had filled itself at that urn, at the risk of life, and in the presence of all the forms of martyrdom, it breathed the spirit of its fountain and its fate.

Now, this is just what is wanted in the world at present: an abounding of hope, which cannot be overlooked, nor passed by unquestioned, nor be suspected of vanity or imbecility. And, surely, if it could abound equally "in all boldness," and "in all wisdom and prudence," on the banks of the river of life, even when the waters reflected the flash of hostile arms, and the glare of threatening flames, it need not tremble, nor temporize, nor vapor, now that the sword is sheathed, and the fire quenched. Why, then, is there so little of this "good hope through grace," to be seen or heard of, in the churches, the families, and the social circles, of the pious? The grace which warrants it is not less full or free now, than it was when Christian hope amazed the world. And yet, the degree of hope usually taken from that grace now arrests no public attention, and creates but little private inquiry. Children do not hear it from their parents nor servants from their masters, nor friends from each other. Even husband and wife hardly venture to breathe it in a whisper to each other. Indeed, were not what is preached and written on the hope of glory illustrated from time to time by happy death-beds, much of it would be unintelligible; so little is there said or done to illustrate it in the ordinary intercourse of life.

"The death of the righteous" does still, however, prove to the world that there is hope in the church; and that "hope maketh not ashamed," when the last struggle comes. I beg your best attention to this fact: that you may not suppose that there is no hope in the church, or that what there is is useless. There is enough to maintain the credit of Christianity as the only antidote against the fear of death. Christians may carry their silence up to the very entrance of the valley of the shadow of death; but they do not pass "through" it in silence. Hope finds it tongue and its harp, too, when in the valley. This is so common, in the case of consistent believers, that the old challenge—*"Mark the perfect man, and behold the upright, for the end of that man is peace,"* —may be safely given to all the world, and unhesitatingly coupled with a defiance to all to find one instance of an upright man dying in horror, or despair, or darkness, when his disease left his faculties unimpaired in their rational exercise. Accordingly, even the Balaams of gain and gaiety do not question the fact that the righteous hath hope in his death. They even keep up the prayer, *"Let me die the death of the righteous, and let my last end be like his."* Why is this prayer thus kept up in the world? Obviously, because the church keeps up an everlasting succession of death-beds, where the sting of death is lost, and the victory of the grave forgotten; and because these signal triumphs over the king of terrors cannot be entirely overlooked or forgotten by mankind. They are not, indeed, much looked at, nor often remembered, from choice: but necessity keeps them in sight. The world cannot afford to forget them. See, how it repeats the last words of Addison, "Behold how calmly a Christian can die." Even in the theatre, where amusement is the sole object and all things are of the earth, earthy; neither the vicious nor the vain can help responding with applause to the exclamation,

"There is another and a better world!"

Not that they love that world: but they all fear death, and cannot suppress the desire of future happiness. No man can, at all times, whatever be his tastes or pursuits. The worse these are, the weaker he is when he looks the last enemy in the face. His own face may not betray this secret, and his lips may deny the fact; but he feels it, however he may mask or vapor, smile or swear. The mortality of his body necessitates this mood of the spirit, when decay begins: and where vice has hastened that decay, the sinking of the spirit hurries it on, by fits and qualms, which upset all hardihood while they last. Thus the world can no more afford to lose sight of all the instances of hope in death, than the church could afford to do so. Very few of them, and these not the best, suffice for the world, to talk about: but still, it must have one or more to quote, whenever it must say something about death, or listen to the voice of nature within. Indeed, mankind are rather glad than otherwise to know that many "depart in peace." The bare fact is, however, enough for the generality. They take no interest in the grounds of that peace, and would hardly listen to the details of it.

As peace founded on the blood of the cross, or confirmed by the witness of the Sprit, or perfected by foretastes of heaven, many would laugh at it: but, simply as peace in death, they are pleased to hear of it. It gets such another place in the temples of taste, fashion and trade, as the Romans would have given to a Phidian statue of Christ in the

Pantheon of their idols. I thus apprize you of the precise temperament of mankind on the subject of exchanging worlds. No man is always nor altogether at ease in his own mind. Every man has his awful moments in spite of himself. His "flesh" will not let him alone, even if his "spirit" would spare him. His constitution breaks down, even if his conscience does not break out upon him. It cannot be otherwise, whilst man is mortal! This is no sweeping assertion. If it seem so to you, you have not looked attentively at the world. True; you see the crowd on "the broad way," keep up its numbers, and its noise, and its pursuits, as if all was ease and enjoyment. The places of those who sink or retire are so soon filled up, that you can hardly distinguish the change of persons. But there is a change of persons forever going on.

Now, if you will mark and follow into retirement those who can no longer keep their wonted place in the crowd, you will soon discover that "the way of transgressors is hard," and that, however they have figured in the world, a time comes when they are tired out, and must retreat; when their hearts ache, and misgive them; when their sins drop the mask, and disgust them; when an earthly portion is felt to be an empty portion; when conscience will not lie still, nor the visions of eternity depart at a bidding. To this point all men come at last; and alas, when they are here, there is, in general, little access to them. Dying Christians cannot be taken to them, to exemplify hope in death: living Christians are seldom admitted to them to explain the way of salvation; and they themselves can make nothing of Addison's example, nor of dramatic sentimentalities on the subject of peace or hope in death. Thus, they have to die as they can, or just as it happens, and whether that be in agony, or in stupor, it is a fool's death.

If ever the world, therefore, is to be savingly benefited by the church, more than "hope in death" must be exemplified in the church: for the multitude cannot be admitted, nor the trifling enticed into *"The chamber where the good man meets his fate."*

It is as much as a dying Christian can well bear, to see his own family and his intimate friends. Thus the world is inevitably shut out from witnessing the best triumphs of hope. It can only hear that there is a victory within. All the impression made upon the actual spectators by beholding a Christian in the valley of the shadow of death, filling up the intervals of pain with angel-like praise or child-like prayer; breathing no murmurs, even in the paroxysms of his agony; betraying no reluctance to leave time, and no fears of facing eternity; and, at last, falling "asleep in Jesus," as if fanned asleep by seraphic wings: all this, and the impression it makes, is lost to the world.

Unless, therefore, Christian hope is allowed and made to "shine before men," where they can all see it and examine it, it cannot tell effectually nor widely. Besides, its final triumphs, however true and frequent, if not preceded by some tokens of present enjoyment from religion, will give currency to the delusion that the death of the righteous may be secured at last by a dying effort without living the life of the righteous. Thus, by suppressing her hope, or by having too little to show, the church practically, however unintentionally, connives at errors which all her creed condemns.

This matter now wears a serious aspect to all who are concerned to stand clear of blood-guiltiness, when they stand confronted with the souls of their neighbors, at the bar of God. It is not impossible, however, to clear ourselves of the blood of all men with whom we have any intercourse. Our responsibilities do not involve violations of the charities or the courtesies of life. It was not by intruding themselves upon the privacy of their neighbors, nor by forcing their religious opinions into the business of the world, that the first Christians discharged their conscience. They cherished all the hope warranted by the gospel, and modelled their character by that hope, and stood prepared to give a reason for all the grace and glory they expected; and this line of conduct led men to inquire about a gospel which had such a holy and happy influence upon its adherents. Thus, their hopes created both opportunities and facilities for winning souls. Now it is no great hardship, surely, to be bound, to take up a hope full of present grace and future glory. It may not, at first sight, seem easy to hope for all that God has promised;

but it is really easier to do so than to keep up a hope only half-full of immortality. That does not make Christ sufficiently precious to the soul, nor set the soul to "look into" all the fullness of the love of Christ: whereas the man who embraces the prospect of all the grace and glory of the new covenant must acquaint himself well with the Mediator of that covenant; and when He is well known as the end of the law for righteousness, and as the author of eternal redemption, to all that believe Him to be so, it is much easier to hope for all the great salvation than it is to hesitate between hope and despair; because the fullness of hope sends the soul directly and fully to all the fullness of Christ.

Now we are warranted to pray for all, and to expect all that Christ has provided for happiness in this life, and in that which is to come. The gospel does not present a title to heaven unto one, and but a peradventure of heaven unto another; does not invite one class to a lively hope, and another to a languid hope, of eternal life. It opens all the riches of the new covenant on earth, and all the beatific vision of the New Jerusalem in heaven, to all men alike. You are, therefore, just as welcome to embrace the whole, as you are warranted to expect any part of the great salvation. Nothing but the blood of Christ warrants any hope; and that blood warrants unbounded hope of all needful grace, and of all revealed glory.

Now with such a hope, do you not see and feel, how, it must give a tone to your spirit and conversation, and a character to your doing and suffering, that could not be overlooked nor laughed at? Whining or canting talk about heaven is a most un-heavenly thing; but when actions speak; when temper speaks; when integrity speaks —when patience speaks of heaven—the world will both look and listen with respect. They know the worth of sterling honesty, and they feel their own want of contentment and peace of mind; and therefore when they see these things based upon a bright eternity, and yet leaning naturally and prudently upon all the helps of reason, law, and religion, they cannot suppress all curiosity, nor forget the sight. Even the infidel press of France could not pass by without notice, the simple-hearted but solemn remark of a French Christian, who said, on refusing to be a party to some questionable transaction in business, "I could never forget it, nor forgive myself, even in heaven."

And, why should not every Christian refer, with as much simplicity, to his anticipations of his eternal opinions and prospects? Where is the real difficulty of having his immortal hopes as closely around him as his moral principles; that thus he might see at a glance how any act or habit of this life will look during the untold and interminable cycles of the life to come? He is not ashamed to base upon law, conscience, and character, refusals to sin or circumvent. He dare not conceal from the world his subjection to moral obligation. And he ought not to conceal the fact that his immortal hopes, as well as his moral principles, influence all his transactions.

Not, however, by the manifestation of such a hope, does the church now try to win the world. And yet, she is neither idle nor indifferent; neither illiberal nor unenterprising at present. All real Christians are doing something, both at home and abroad, to win souls. Ingenuity is taxed to simplify and adapt the stores of knowledge to minds of all orders and conditions of all grades. Benevolence provides something for all kinds of misery, and philanthropy espouses the cause of all the oppressed. History begins to remember the forgotten, and to vindicate the calumniated martyrs of civil and religious liberty. Even poetry pays some homage to the genius of Christianity, and is compelled to pitch her key-note in harmony with the tone of Christian morals. No bench dare avow infidelity, nor any senator assail the Bible. Even the press must bow to the majesty of revelation, however it may tamper with some revealed truths. Now, all this influence the church of the living God has put forth upon the world. Yes; Christians have done it in this country. It has been their influence, however unacknowledged or unseen, that has kept the march of intellect upon the highways of truth; that has kept the streams of knowledge in the channels of virtue; that has kept the progress of liberty on the side of religion.

MANLY PIETY IN ITS SPIRIT

Things are not so in France. No political movement there has led to any great moral result, even when the policy was wise, and the public spirit noble in themselves. Why? There was not Christianity enough in France to regulate or influence the movements. They had not only no immortal hope to center in, but no moral system to support. Indeed, they had nothing to terminate upon but just the temporal purposes for which they were undertaken: and no liberty can be lasting, nor satisfactory whilst it lasts, which is not made to bear upon the glory of God, and the eternal welfare of mankind. I thus refer to the influence of Christian principle on the spirit and manners of the age at home, to prove that the Church of Christ is neither inactive nor useless. She makes herself felt, if not heard, in all the assemblies and associations of the land. They do not and dare not forget that there is holy fire upon ten thousand of her altars, and millions of holy men within her spiritual pale, who would guard these altars with their life, if that fire were in danger. This is much: but it is not enough. It tells widely and well upon morals, and legislation, and social order; but not directly upon the human heart. It is a mighty impulse upon masses of society; but not upon individual men.

Individuals must act upon individuals, if ever personal religion become universal. The great charm of true religion is the happiness it confers: and that happiness cannot be fully seen in the fellowship of a church, nor even in the peace of a family. There is, indeed, happiness in both these spheres; but not that precious form of it, which every man appreciates at first sight, and which all men feel their need of at times. The fact is, (and it is solemn enough to be repeated) every man is occasionally a wretched man. Whatever may be his tastes or pursuits, and however he may appear satisfied or absorbed with them, there are moments of satiety, of disgust, of heart-sickness and heart-sinking, which compel him to confess to himself that he is wretched: that neither gain nor gaiety has answered his expectations; that all is vanity and vexation of spirit! Now, during these awful moments and humiliating emotions, recollections of God and eternity do force themselves in upon the conscience. Their terrific flash may be as momentary as the glare of the midnight thunderbolt; but it is as startling too, while it lasts, and not entirely forgotten when it is gone. The man himself can see the traces of it on his brow in the morning, although no one else can detect them. He feels also more than the bad headache, or the sleepless night, he complains of: his soul is as feverish as his body. Now it is that form of happiness which could remove this gnawing uneasiness, and prevent its return, that such a man requires to see: but that form of happiness—he cannot see, if there be no one in the circle of his acquaintance manifesting the beauty of hope, as well as the beauty of holiness.

Why should not these twin-beauties be combined in your character? You know young men and old men too, who are unhappy. You are sure from their habits that they cannot be otherwise than wretched, at times; and you see that they will not brook reproof nor warning. Must they, therefore, be left to perish? At your peril—do not allow yourself to regard your old school-fellow, or former friend, as hopeless. He may have lost his character; but he has not lost sight of you, even if he shun you. It may be unsafe for you to associate with him much or openly; but, as you do cross each other's path from time to time, you can, by acquiring and manifesting a hope full of immortality, awaken his curiosity to the secret of your personal happiness. Do "clothe" yourself with hope, as well as with "humility." You may thus save more souls than your own.

In order to do this, however, you must set yourself to acquire first a clear understanding of the nature of faith. You cannot hope well until you believe aright. Perhaps, the next essay will assist your faith and hope. It will, at least, enable you to think for yourself upon a subject of supreme importance, which is too often mystified by talkers and speculators.

4

Of Manly Views of Avowals of Faith

Faith is as much the first and chief principle of all the business of life, as it is of all the duties of godliness. No men act more by faith, in pursuing their temporal avocations and objects, than those who speak most against faith as the grand principle of religion. The glaring inconsistency would be ludicrous, were not its consequences fatal. It is, however, *"passing strange,"* that men who can neither live nor move without faith in men and things, should yet make light of faith, when God and truth, salvation and eternity, are the objects of it. These solemn and sublime objects deserve, surely, quite as much faith as the temporal things which make both public, and social life "a life of faith," in the order of nature—in the laws of nations—in the grounds of commerce, and in the promises of mankind. The confidence given to these things may not, indeed, be always called faith (although even that is its usual name both in trade and treaties), but it really is faith. How, then, would the mockers at religious faith like to be pitied or despised for their faith in food and medicine—in bills and bonds—in ships and mails—in banks and firms? They can neither trade nor travel without faith. They buy and sell by faith. They eat and drink by faith. In a word, they can do no business without it, nor have any enjoyment apart from it: for were they to give up their faith in the ordinary integrity of mankind, or in the nutrition of the fruits of the earth, they must give up too both the means and the pursuits of life. And yet, men of business, and men of pleasure, and even literary men, can so far forget all the decencies of common sense and decorum, as to laugh at faith, or try to be witty at its expense, when it is enforced as the first and chief thing in religion.

Is this manly or fair? I will not retaliate upon them by ridiculing their strong faith in each other, and in all the general laws which regulate human policy, trade, enterprise, and social life. Natural, national, and mutual faith is too essential to the welfare of mankind, to be less than sacred in the estimation of a Christian. The world may laugh at his faith in the things which are unseen and eternal; but he will not make light of their faith in the things which are seen and temporal. I do, however, claim the right of telling the world in plain terms, that they play with a two-edged sword, when they make light of divine faith. If they do not know, they ought to know, that divine faith is just such a degree of confidence in divine things, as they themselves give to temporal things, and expect to get from Christians in the business of life. Is, therefore, they would not teach us to distrust themselves, and to treat all their own veracity as doubtful, why should they arraign, as useless or visionary, our faith in the character and word of God? For, if there be any' thing weak in the habit of trusting Him, there must be egregious folly in trusting them. If there be nothing wrong nor rash in disbelieving God, there can be no great harm in disbelieving any man and every man. You cannot dislike this "retort courteous;" and yet, perhaps, you do not see clearly the analogy between human and divine faith. You may even suspect that the parallels would not hold good, but break down, if it were pursued very far: and thus you may feel afraid to employ the argument. Look, however, at the facts again.

You know the confidence which farmers have in the order of nature, and merchants in commercial treaties, and all men in established capital and character. There are momentary panics in all the markets; but business still goes on somewhere. Now, did the farmer place as much confidence in the promise of the renewing and sanctifying influences of the Holy Spirit, as he gives to the promise of "the early and latter rain," would not that be faith in God? And, did the merchant repose only as much confidence in the Savior, as he places in his bankers and agents, would not that be faith in Christ? I do not, of course, mean that it would be all the faith which God and the Lamb demand and deserve. It would, however, be some; and so much as must lead to more. And, let any man who has entire confidence in any human security, give entire confidence to divine promises, what would that be, but "strong faith"? Thus all the difference between natural and divine faith is made by the difference between human and divine things, and by the difference there is between human and divine agency.

It is not, however, by any new or occult mental faculty that a man begins to believe the gospel; but by new motives and influences acting on his old faculties. He them believes eternal things, just as he had before believed temporal things. His faith is no longer confined to this world but extends to the eternal world. It has new objects, and quite another kind of influence than it had, whilst it terminated on the things of time and sense: but it is not a new mental process. It is still the old or natural act of believing, drawn out and led on by the Spirit of God, to new and nobler truths and purposes.

A true believer is, therefore, just thinking, and reasoning, and judging, and trusting, as naturally, and freely, as to the mental process in the case of eternal things, as worldly-wise men do in the case of earthly things. I mean he is not doing more or otherwise in regard to eternity, than they are doing in regard to time. Alas, the only difference is that he does less in the work of believing God, than they do in the work of believing man. It is, therefore, no more weak, visionary, fanatical, or irrational, to extend *"a strong and lasting faith,"* to all revealed truth, than it is to believe the ascertained facts of science and history, or the pledged word of well accredited men.

"If we receive the witness of men, the witness of God is greater;" greater in itself, and in all that it testifies. This view of faith, and the argument founded upon it, being derived from the express "words which the

Holy Ghost teacheth," cannot be at variance with the work of the Holy Ghost in producing faith. The line of argument is at variance only with those vague and mystical motions about faith which perplex the serious, and harden the slothful. Faith is, indeed, "not of ourselves: it is the gift of God; a fruit of the Spirit;" an effect of "divine operation." It is also, however, the duty of man. If it were not, unbelief would not be a sin, and especially not the condemning sin. That, however, it is; and, therefore, we are as much accountable for our faith as for our practice. No wonder: the grounds of accountability for what and how we believe are as firmly laid in the everlasting gospel, as the grounds of it for what and how we obey are laid in the eternal law.

The gospel presents truth to us as clearly as the law presents duty; and, therefore, it demands faith, just as the law demands obedience; and with equal reason too. Law is the judicial will of God: Gospel is the gracious will of God; and, surely, it cannot be less our duty or interest to believe the latter than it is to obey the former. The former reveals to us the legislative character of God, and the latter His paternal character: and as He has condescended to sustain all the pity and love of a Father towards the human family, notwithstanding all their guilt and ingratitude, well may He expect and demand that they should believe this fact with the heart, and give implicit credit and entire confidence to its revealed reasons and designs.

Let no man deceive you, neither let your own sloth betray you into quibbles about faith. The impossibility of believing the gospel without the grace of the Holy Spirit is exactly such an impossibility as the growth of grain, without sunshine and showers: it no more sets aside or lessens your obligation to "sow unto the Spirit," than the other absolves the farmer from the duty of ploughing and sowing his fields. The influences of the Spirit in producing faith are like the influences of the heavens in producing corn: neither supply seed, nor supplant human labor; and both operate agreeably to the nature of the seed and the soil. Nothing, therefore, can be more absurd or impertinent, than to plead as an apology for the want of faith, that the Holy Spirit has not given you grace to believe. What do you wish to believe, if not the gospel? He gives no grace to believe anything else. And, if it be the gospel you wish to believe with the heart, acquaint yourself with it, if you would have Him to work mightily or effectually. His grace gives power to His truth.

What attention, then, do you give to the gospel itself? I mean, to the gospel, as "glad news" from heaven to earth. It is, indeed a system of truth, as opposed to error; and a system of morality, as opposed to vice; and a system of worship, as opposed to idolatry and superstition; and a system of grace, as opposed to merit: but it is all this just because it is glad tidings of a great salvation; and, therefore, it is not heard or read aright, until heard and read as good news in a bad world, or as a message of tender mercy, direct from the eternal throne, to the unworthy. Now, is it thus you have attended to the glorious gospel of the blessed God. You may have studied it as a creed—as a controversy— as a system of faith and practice; but if you have not weighed it as "the joyful sound" of a pardon you need— of a deliverance from wrath you deserve—of a title to glory you desire—you have not yet treated it as gospel, but as law, or as advice, or as theology. This is the chief reason why so many who hear the gospel with some attention and much respect yet remain, year after year, without the Spirit. They hear—as judges of sound doctrine; as friends of good morals; as umpires between orthodoxy and heresy; as men of sense, or men of science, or men of taste, or men of business, or as family men;–but not as sinners, who deserve none of the mercy they need.

Now, how can the Spirit of God be expected to countenance this spirit in man? As the Spirit of truth, He is not indifferent to the fear of error: as the Spirit of holiness, not indifferent to the love of virtue: as the Spirit of wisdom, not indifferent to good sense or good taste: but He is also "the Spirit of Christ;" and as His grand object is to glorify Christ as a Savior from hell and sin, how can He follow with a saving blessing any attention to the gospel which is not for the sake of an immediate salvation from the wrath to come?

Here, now, is the point. If you are concerned only about a remote or final salvation, you are offering a present insult to the God of salvation: for He beseeches you to be reconciled to Him now, because "now" is the only day of salvation that you can calculate upon as "the accepted time." You are offering a present insult to the Lamb of God: for although He "now liveth to intercede," He has made no promise to take up your case at a future period. A regard only to a remote salvation, is, also, a present insult to the Spirit of God: for "the Holy Ghost saith, today, if ye will hear My voice." Thus remote intentions, however good or sincere, are present insults to Father, Son, and Holy Ghost: and can the Spirit countenance such conduct? Is it any wonder that He does not give grace to help, whilst there is no intention of making a present use of it? Why should He—or, indeed, how could He, work faith in your heart, if you have no wish nor design to exercise it until you are older or in greater danger of death?

I do not forget the sovereignty of the Spirit's influences. That sacred "wind bloweth" both when and where it listeth. But I remember also that it is not promised to blow at all upon any one who hears the gospel merely as a present creed, or as a future command. Besides, if you can judge of its claims to credence, as doctrine; and of its beauty, as morality; and of its sublimity, as philosophy; and of its truth, as history—you can do more than all this; you can weigh its claims upon yourself, as a sinner and a candidate for eternity: for you have a conscience as well as an understanding: and as you would not dare to silence your reason, nor your taste, nor your judgment, when the truth, beauty, and holiness of Christianity are brought before you, why should you not allow your conscience to speak out, when the refuge and remedy of the gospel are commended? You yourself see and feel that it would be an insult to the Holy Spirit to expect Him to countenance levity or willful ignorance. You do not expect that, nor wish for it. You are not unwilling to let the general truths of the gospel have a fair hearing, nor to allow them to have some weight on your mind, and some influence on your character. Nothing you know or feel about your need of grace, leads you to lay aside your talents, when you read or hear the gospel. Why, then, lay aside your conscience? I mean—why not let it speak out, when the necessity and suitableness of saving blessings are proved, as well as let reason speak out when the truth of Christianity is proved?

The chief value of the historical truth of the gospel, is, that it justifies faith in its joyful sound: and, as conscience can judge as well of the goodness of the glad news of salvation, as reason can of their truth, it is as criminal not to employ conscience, as it is not to employ common sense. Let conscience speak now. It is not altogether easy. It is not without some fears and forebodings. There is more guilt upon it than you would like your friends or the world to know. That guilt, even after all your own softenings and subterfuges, casts a dark shadow upon the swellings of Jordan, and upon the judgment-seat beyond them. You cannot contemplate, with anything like composure, the opening of "the books" on the great white throne. Although not worse than many, and even better than some, you are conscious that you are not prepared to meet God, nor yet to inherit glory. There is thus darkness upon your future prospects, and suspense on your spirit. And, then, you see, what many do not look at—that it will require strong faith, "some day," to get over such fears. Accordingly, you intend, what many do not, to make a believing application to the blood of atonement, for pardon and acceptance. You have no intention of risking your soul, at last, upon a late repentance or a legal reformation. You design and desire to be indebted to Christ for salvation, whenever you proceed to act out your convictions of truth and duty. Thus, your conscience has already discovered that it will want the glad tidings of the gospel; and is now somewhat gladdened, to remember that there is something in the cross worth looking at and relying on.

And are you not as much bound to apply this conscience to the study of the gospel's worthiness of all acceptance, as to apply your understanding to the faithfulness of its testimony? You say to yourself, "I am a rational being, and must not reject evidence: I am an accountable being, and must not trifle with truth: I am a mortal being, and must not entirely peril myself, in time or eternity:" but, why not add, "I am a guilty being, and need pardon now: I am an unholy being, and need sanctification now." This is equally true, and far more solemn than the general fact that it is wrong to be irreligious. And, do you not see that this way of attending to the gospel is just the way to meet the Holy Spirit? He can own and honor such consideration of the things which belong to your peace: whereas, whilst you consider them only as they belong to your talents, and taste, and character, He cannot witness, and has not promised to work with you.

True; He wrought mightily upon those who first heard the gospel, although they had not gone through any such process of thought as I am now enforcing upon you. At Pentecost, and on other occasions of apostolic preaching, thousands were led into the faith of the gospel, as fast as they acquired the knowledge of it. They heard with the ear, and were enabled to believe with the heart, on the same day. I will not evade this fact by calling it miraculous. If, however, you mean to insinuate that those who believed then went through no process of consideration beforehand, you have yet to study the apostolic history of both the Jews and the Gentiles. That the first converts went through no such process as I commend to you, is indeed, quite certain. But, remember, all Judea had been shaken by the fear of the wrath to come, under the rousing ministry of John the Baptist; and all the people of Jerusalem, who beheld the solemnities of Calvary, "smote their breasts and returned." Was this no preparation for Pentecost? Thus, so far as Jews believed on that day, they had both thought and felt, too, beforehand.

And as to the Gentiles, you may well be thankful that you have no such process of thought or feeling to go through as heathenism forced upon them. That was not, indeed, a softening process, any farther than suffering tends to soften the heart; and that is not far, when nothing else co-operates. Still, misery, as well as meditation, is calculated to prepare the mind for the glad tidings of eternal happiness. Wretchedness, as well as reflection, can draw attention to good news and teach something of the value of a remedy. Now, wretchedness must have been as common as vice throughout the heathen world. This is no conjecture. The time is gone by, when a sciolist could dupe the common sense of mankind by pictures of happiness amongst idolaters. It is now an ascertained fact (as might have been anticipated, from the very nature of the human mind), that no heathen nation is happy. The most ignorant and savage are found to be restless, even when reckless. A mysterious dread haunts the spirit of the hunter in the wilderness, and of the cannibal of the islands. Yea, they seek more than the gratification of appetite, when they sell everything for intoxicating liquors. Their craving for excitement is not simply animal desire; there is conscience in it, although they cannot define it, nor we analyze it. How much more must this have been the case, amongst the civilized heathen of Greece and Rome?

He sees only the surface of men and things, who does not feel that the very splendor of heathen temples, altars, and sacrifices, is as much the measure of the people's consciousness of guilt and fear, as it is the measure of their vanity, folly, taste, or genius. Men never impoverish nor tax themselves for any religion without a moral reason based in the fears and misgivings of their hearts. God, who knows "what is in man," has assured us, that they were "without hope in the world;" that they were all "their lifetime in bondage, through fear of death." Now, this, with the uncertainty and practical inefficiency which hung over all their loftiest speculations, formed, not indeed, a softening process of preparation for the gospel, but still, a preparation; inasmuch as it was experience of the insufficiency of all human things to confer happiness. Thus, you have no reason to grudge the thought or prayer, which your better circumstances render the best process for obtaining grace. It is an easy process, compared with the remorse of the Jews, or with the bitter experience of the Gentiles.

Remember, therefore, that both had been on the rack of suspense and fear, before they heard the gospel; and that this is one reason why so many of them "received the word gladly," when they first heard it. This, indeed, was not the only nor the chief reason of their prompt and cordial belief of the gospel. That was emphatically the fruits of the

Spirit; but still not apart from the means of grace or from the measures of Providence. Divine influence did not follow those who fled from the preaching of the gospel, nor act on those who braved all the discipline of Providence. Having thus seen that it is no part of the Spirit's work to implant new faculties, nor to set aside the use of scriptural or rational means in order to our believing aright; you may now see clearly how our natural power of believing testimony in general, becomes the principle of divine faith, whenever it is honestly and prayerfully applied to the belief of the divine testimony concerning Christ and salvation. Then, just as natural tears become penitential when they flow from a sense of the evil of sin; and just as natural sounds become devotion when they are breathed from the heart; and just as natural smiles becomes the visible joy of salvation when the soul is happy in Christ, so natural faith becomes divine faith when it believes divine and eternal things; because that exercise of our natural power is always crowned by the saving blessings of the eternal Spirit.

You may have heard, or you may yet be told, that you cannot act honestly nor seriously in trying to believe the gospel until you are acted upon by the Holy Spirit. There are not a few well-meaning, as well as ill-meaning men who talk in this way; and, therefore, that you may not confound them together when they attempt to confuse you, I will deal very tenderly with this objection. Now, without going into the abstract question of how much or how little you can do before you are acted upon by the Holy Spirit—just look at what you have done, already, in believing the gospel; for already you believe parts of it. So far as its historical truth, and its holy design, and some of its doctrines are concerned, it has won your faith. Well; you have believed thus far either with or without the help of the Spirit. By some means, you have gone beyond both Infidels and Jews, and identified yourself to a great extent with true believers, so far as the general truth of the gospel is concerned. Now, if you do not ascribe, or ought not to ascribe, this degree of faith to the work of the Holy Spirit upon your heart—then, thus much you were able, of yourself, or without the Spirit, to believe: for you have

MANLY PIETY IN ITS SPIRIT

done it. I do not say that you have done it without His help. All I say, at present is that thus far you have believed: and, if you cannot trace it to a higher power, then, it is a specimen of your own power, as a rational being. And, if of your power, it is also, of course, a specimen of any man's and every man's power, who is rational.

Now, we shall get at the facts in this matter. You have done wrong, so far as you have overlooked the office and influences of the Holy Spirit, whilst acquainting yourself with the doctrines and duties of the gospel: but you have done right, so far as you have acquainted yourself with the claims of truth and duty. You might, however, have given as much attention to the work of the Spirit as to the word of God. You were as capable of reading "Owen on the Spirit," as of reading Paley's or Chalmer's Evidences. And, do you not see, in the very attention you are now giving to this essay, that you have as much power to think of divine influence, as of divine truth? Let no man, therefore, palm off on you the pretense that you can do nothing in believing the gospel until you are conscious of the work of the Spirit upon your heart. You have refuted the pretense by what you have done. Yes, and he who would teach you this pretense refutes himself by expecting you to believe it. For, whether he give you credit for power to understand and believe his statements, or hope that his statements may be blessed to you, he is, in fact, claiming from you as much attention to his own theory as I am claiming for the gospel. Men who talk in this way, about the necessity of the work of the Spirit, utter, what they reckon, a cardinal truth of the gospel. Ask them, therefore, why they address it to you? If they say "because you can or may understand and believe it," they ascribe to you, and make you responsible for, as much power as I do. And if, on the other hand, they say that "all their hope of its doing you any good, is, that the Spirit works by means," then, they contradict their own theory, and throw open the whole system of means to your activity: for, surely, if you are bound to make a good use of their hints it can neither be optional nor useless to improve all means.

But I would rather reason with you than against such men. Now you can (and you know it) believe God, just as well, and as far, as you believe man. Of course, therefore, thus far, and thus well, you are bound to believe God. To say or think otherwise would be equally absurd and impious: absurd, because what you really do in giving credit to human testimony, you certainly can do in the case of divine testimony: impious, because if any human word deserve your faith, not to give it to the word of God is to put him on a level with liars. To say, therefore, that you cannot give as much faith to what God declares as you do give to what honest men promise would be a greater contradiction in terms than to say that you could not give equal faith to men equally honest. You can believe any number of equally upright men; and, thus far at least, you can believe "God who cannot lie."

Have you, then, believed Him thus far, and thus well? Do not evade this question, by asking, whether this would be far enough, and well enough to amount to saving faith. For, what if it fell far short of that? What if saving faith did not even begin until this was done? This ought to be done, and this you are as able to do, as you are able to believe two witnesses of equal veracity. This, however, you have not done yet, nor tried to do, on all the points on which "the Mighty God, the Lord, hath spoken." On some of the great truths of the gospel, you agree with Him: on others you are afraid to differ from Him: but some of its truths you have not yet brought home to yourself, nor seriously examined. Now, whatever these neglected truths may be, and whether neglected from dislike or oversight, you are criminal in thus neglecting them: because you were just as capable of considering them as you were of weighing those which you do believe. I have told you plainly, some parts of the gospel you have not set yourself to believe yet: and I must point out others, before this question can be brought to an issue. In the meantime, however, I remind you that you have not believed God where He says, that "now" only, is, certainly, the accepted time, or the day of salvation. You have believed that a future time would do well enough for your day of salvation; and even yet, you are induced to ask, will it not answer the purpose? Here, then, is one point on which you disbelieve God. But you do not mean to say, surely, that you cannot believe Him on this point?

"Now" may not, indeed, be the only day on which you could obtain salvation; but as it is the only day you can call your own, or that you are authorized to calculate upon, all your obligations to seek an interest in Christ center in this day, because all your opportunities of doing so may expire with it. And yet, still you hesitate to make an immediate application to the Savior for eternal life. This hesitation, in a matter of such infinite moment, arises from not believing God fully on another solemn point—the extent of your demerit and danger, as a sinner. For, although you believe that you are in some danger, and that you cannot merit salvation, you do not believe that you are in great or immediate danger of losing your soul. But why not? If because you think that it would hardly be fair, or that it would be harshly just, to cut short your probation by early death, or by judicial blindness: then, you either do not believe God when He says that salvation is wholly of grace, or you do not believe Him when he says that His long-suffering is exercised not to delay repentance, but to lead to repentance. Thus you disbelieve Him, whether you imagine that you have any claim, in justice, upon grace, or upon a long day of grace; that you run but little risk in taking liberties with His long-suffering: for all His word declares that you have no personal right to the grace you need, or to the time you would take.

Observe also, how much you disbelieve God when he says that "all" his "paths are peace." In regard to some of the paths of duty, you doubt the truth of this declaration. You do not believe that it would increase your present happiness to "follow the Lord fully." There is something in which you now take pleasure that you deem more pleasant than full consecration to God. Here again you are at issue with Him, although He has solemnly assured you that *"the ways of wisdom are ways of pleasantness, and all her paths peace."* But there would be no end to this process of search for unbelief. All preferences of earthly to heavenly things, and all pretenses for delay, are just the measure of your remaining unbelief. They are not, however, the sole causes of it. You have not set yourself to the task of believing God on the points where you differ from Him or doubt his word. You have not tried to conquer your aversions or evasions, your doubts or delays, by confronting them one by one with all the testimony of God and all the solemnity of eternity. You have even left some of your tendencies to trifle and compromise to take their own way. You have not only not brought them under the full light of divine truth, but you have kept out that light, that you might not see all their sinfulness and folly. Thus, in some things you have not believed God because you have "not come to the light" which unmasks unbelief. But you can "come to the light" on these points; for you have come to it on other points. All that you believe on the subject of sin and holiness, of salvation and eternity, is from the attention you have given to the divine testimony. You would not have believed as you do, had you not read and reflected as you have dome. Why, then, should you stop this process, now that you see your unbelief taking its stand upon the perilous ground of presumptuous delay? For all delay is presumption. What else, or less could it be?

Now, if you dare not allow unbelief to take its stand against truth in general, upon the ground of mystery nor upon the ground of divisions in the church, nor upon the ground of aversions to moral restraint—why allow it to take its stand against the particular truth—that there is no time, certainly a day of salvation, but the present time—upon the presumption that a future time will do as well? You can, by reading and reflection, reason yourself out of this presumption. One hour of meditation and prayer against it would upset it; and the repetition of this process for a week would destroy it. You know—you feel—that it could not stand long before a decided attempt to put it down. You are not, therefore, thoroughly in earnest about the safety of your soul, if you grudge or hesitate to try this process. It is even unmanly to delay longer the full improvement of your natural powers and religious opportunities. For, see what you allow to prevent it!

"Tell it not in Gath—publish it not in the streets of Askelon," that you, who will not allow vice to enslave you, nor infidel sophistry to seduce you, nor the world to divert you altogether from religion, yet succumb to the hollow plausibility of a hasty presumption that the day of your merciful visitation will last until you choose to fix your own "convenient season." Nor is this all that is mean and weak, in delaying to go all the length in believing, which God has gone in testifying; and all the length in obeying, which God has gone in commanding. You are standing out now, for reasons which you know you must one day give up; which you intend to give up; yea, and to repent of having ever given way to them. Is this manly? It is as weak as it is wicked; you yourself being judge. Now, what power, but that of the Holy Spirit, can effectually dislodge all this unbelief? And what means, but trying to believe, can he be expected to work by? There can be no such thing as faith, apart from the knowledge of the truths to be believed; and knowledge of them all can only be acquired by attention to them all: and, as you are quite as capable of acquainting yourself with the parts of the gospel you have hitherto evaded as you were of studying those which you have believed, your duty is obvious; *"whereunto you have attained; walk by the same rule, mind the same things."* Let this be your rule, whoever rail or pity. Tell any man and every man who admits that it is your duty to read and hear the word of God, that it must be your duty to weigh it also, as well as you can; and to believe it as much as you are able: for, if neither reading nor hearing it, be a process of trying to do without the Spirit, considering it, is, certainly, not a proud nor a legal process; and praying over it, is anything but dishonoring the Spirit.

Hitherto, this argument has gone forward on the supposition that the Spirit of God has had nothing to do with your faith, thus far. This supposition may, however, be as unfounded as it is gratuitous. Indeed, it is unfounded, if you have ever been deeply affected by any of the great truths of the gospel. Whatever leading part of law or gospel you cannot forget, and dare not try to get over nor resist, has been brought home to your conscience by the Spirit of truth. You never tremble nor wept for yourself under a sermon, nor an affliction, but He had something to do with your serious emotions: both when you could not help praying, and when you found it difficult to extricate yourself from what seemed the grasp of an invisible hand on your soul, drawing you out of the world into your closet. He was striving with you, and stirring you up to flee from the wrath to come.

You are not, therefore, an utter stranger to divine influence. God has left a witness in your heart by His Spirit, as well as in your hands by His word. Nor is this disproved by your delay or indecision, in personal religion. They are, indeed, awfully aggravated by the resistance you have made against your convictions: but they are not proofs that the Spirit had no hand in producing these convictions. Indeed as your own spirit did not seek for them —and as Satan would not have excited them— where could they have come from, but from Him whose office it is, to "convince of sin"? Remember; *"the carnal, or (natural) mind,"* whilst entirely in a state of nature, *"is enmity against God, and mot all subject to the law of God,"* from choice: and therefore, some degree of divine power has operated upon it whenever its enmity to God and law give way at all to the truth of the gospel. Do consider this. It may both lead and warrant you, to say of more spots than Jacob spoke of, *"Verily, God was in this place—although I knew it not."* He was—in all the places, wherever you felt His character, as the God of salvation, to be attractive; or His law to be as "good" as it is holy.

Now see—what encouragements and facilities you have for believing the gospel fully! I mean for believing its "joyful sound." Let nothing divert your attention from its "glad tidings of great joy." Systematize its doctrines into a creed, if you will; or adopt, as your confession of faith, whatever formula you reckon most scriptural; but do not substitute this theologizing for believing the message of mercy which the gospel brings to you. That is your life; and upon it, your faith and hope should fix, as the condemned criminals fix upon the royal message of pardon. That is his first and chief object of attention. He may, afterward, admire the seal and the style of the document; but for a time he is absorbed with the great subject of it. His life was in jeopardy, and his heart in fear; and that relieved both at once. Your soul is in great peril, whether your heart be equally afraid or not; and nothing can relieve either from eternal pain but the cordial belief of the glorious gospel.

Again, I say, "in understanding be men." You cannot but see, that all the truths, which the giddy and the heedless and the heartless refuse to believe now—they must believe when they stand at the bar of God. But then belief can do no good. It can do good now. No one ever tried to believe the Gospel in vain.

5

Of Manly Devotedness to the Divine Glory

"We must run glittering like a brook in the open sunshine,
Or we are unblest."

 This is emphatically true of all minds, and especially of great minds. Great objects are necessary for them. For what purpose? That great minds may not prey upon themselves. Unemployed and misapplied talents are sure to revenge themselves upon their possessors. They will not lie in the mind, like lightning in a cloud, without injuring their sanctuary or losing their energy; but will impair, at once, their shrine and themselves. Great powers were created for great purposes; and, when not applied to them, they assail each other like wild beasts in a cage. Memory keeps conscience sleepless, and imagination torments both. The visions of fancy become the realities of sensation. The brain burns sensibly; and the palpitations of the heart are the pulsations of the soul. Thoughts are substances, and feelings convulsions.

 Men of some talent, and of much taste, when they witness these woes of genius, feel thankful that they themselves are not geniuses; and prefer, infinitely, their own healthy sensations and orderly conceptions to all the sublime flights and brilliant flashes of morbid power. Well they may! An orbit like a comet is indeed fascinating, by the vastness of its sweep, and the variety of its scenery; but a mind with the motion and character of a comet is no enviable distinction. Better shine like the faintest star of the galaxy, than blaze like the meteors of the universe. There is, however, no essential nor inseparable tendency to morbid disease in great mental powers. It is not by any law of their nature that they run wild. Accordingly, when they are so engrossed with great public objects that self is absorbed in pure philanthropy, they work well. The moment a great man ceases to be his own center, he begins to enjoy himself: and whenever he forgets himself on behalf of mankind, his powers move as regularly as the stars in the firmament, without tarnishing the beauty, or disturbing the repose, of their sanctuary. The reason is obvious: they find in real philanthropy, a sphere commensurate with their might, and even surpassing it. It is this that restores and establishes the balance of great mental powers. They cease to be felt, or to appear, too great, whenever the field of moral desolation opens in all its width and woes. Idolatry, slavery, and superstition, when understood, impose upon the mightiest mind—not exactly such a sense of its own weakness as renders their overthrow hopeless; but such a conviction of the inadequacy of all mere human power to overthrow them, as the ocean, in a storm, produces, of the insufficiency of any human power to calm it.

Talents are thus brought to their real level, as well as into their proper element, when fairly confronted with, and committed upon, the grand and eternal interests of the world. It is the too little, not the too much of power, that is then felt. The greatest rocks, in common with "the sands" upon the shores of the aggressive sea of evil, feel their own insufficiency to repel its waves. This is a conviction which nothing else can produce. The ordinary pursuits are so ordinary, that they only inflate the consciousness of mental power. One man could produce sermons which would eclipse all the triumphs of the pulpit; another, which would electrify a public meeting; another, a book which would immortalize him: but they do not. Why? They think it beneath them to appear in the arena of emulation. So it would, if the effect terminated wholly or chiefly in their own fame. To be the first preacher, the first orator, or the first writer, of his age, is a distinction unworthy of a great man to covet on its own account. In this connection, his mind would as soon weary of it, as his head would of wearing the iron crown of Charlemagne. It would be more than an encumbrance: it would prove a curse, by throwing his mighty powers in upon himself, and loose upon each other. He might soon become a dram-drinker, from utter sickness of his own fame. But—let the same man espouse one or more of the grand moral interests of the world at large, and identify his being and his bliss with it, for time and eternity, and make his purpose of carrying it, his fate, and hold it to be himself —what aspect, them, would the pulpit, the platform, and the press wear to him? Not that of arenas to shrink from, or to be ashamed of: but vantage grounds, on which to exhibit, not himself, but prostrate and perishing millions, crying out for liberty and salvation. Let the man who wishes to hide himself put them forward; and he will soon cease to think of himself, or to be thought of, except as their representative.

How impossible it is to conceive of Wilberforce, or Howard, or Martyn, or Bogue, or Fuller, or Hughes, as thinking of himself, or of what others might think of his talents, whilst he was planning and pleading for the welfare of mankind! What fills the public eye or the public ear, when these great names are mentioned? The causes they espoused; the misery they represented; the triumphs they achieved. Wilberforce is only another name for African liberty: Howard, another name for philanthropy; Bogue, and Fuller, and Martyn, and Dr. Philip, other names for missions; and Hughes, for the Bible and Tract Societies. Why, then, are there not more names of note, equally identified with these noble enterprises, and absorbed in them: Oh! It is not a sermon preached officially; nor a speech extorted by force; nor a solitary pamphlet upon an emergency, that amounts to an espousal of the cause of God and man. If that cause be worth anything, it is worth more than countenance, or an occasional official effort. It demands and deserves high and habitual enthronement in the minds of great men. But, alas, it is not thus enthroned by many of them.

In reference to the paramount interest of the world at large, the parable of "The talents" is often reversed. Many who have received "ten talents," bury them in the earth: whilst many, who have but "one talent," gain by its wise application, the plaudit of the judge. Only a few of the great minds of the age are thoroughly engrossed with the great enterprises of the age. Many profound thinkers live only to think. Some of our best writers write least. Most of the fine imaginations waste their creative power upon worthless objects; and, like amber, embalm flies. And, "verily, they have their reward '" In the case of perverted talent, that reward is often fearful. "Weeping and gnashing of teeth" succeed unhallowed speculations; and, occasionally, the "outer darkness" of reason is both the natural and judicial consequence of unholy theorizing. Even "unprofitable servants" do not escape with impunity. They, too, have their depressions and hallucinations; their days of darkness and nights of horror. The lava-flow of their blood, and the soul-withering glare of their visions, are as much realities as the remorse and fear of a guilty conscience. Our sympathy with men of genius, when they suffer thus, must not shut our eyes to the causes of this self-torment. If they have thought deeply only for the sake of deep thinking: or speculated wantonly only to show the strength of their wings; or "meddled with all knowledge," only to prove their power; what else could be expected, but the dislocation of some mental faculty, and the disease of the whole?

It is a mercy to mankind that the perversion of intellectual power disorders or impairs it. Wild and wanton theories are but too abundant, as it is; and, could such men theorize to any extent, without unhinging their own minds, and ruining their own happiness, the public mind would soon be unsettled and poisoned. But "the lusts of the mind," like "the lusts of the flesh," cannot be indulged with impunity. They sap or shatter the mental constitution as effectually and certainly as sensuality undermines the body; and, therefore, their effects should be as freely exposed, that they may operate as warnings.

It is, however, inaction, rather than extravagance, that these hints are intended to bear upon. Perverted genius is almost irreclaimable, because in general, it is irreligious. An irreligious man, however great, cannot serve any good cause effectually. Byron could not have regenerated Greece nor hastened her liberty, however long he had been spared to the cause he espoused, but by abandoning many of his own principles. He must have made real or pretended advances towards the Cross, in a struggle against the Crescent. He could not have raised the throne of liberty, without venerating the altar of religion. The spirit-stirring history of ancient Greece, however appealed to or employed, would not have inspired modern Greeks, apart from the history of Christianity. The poet would have been compelled to accommodate himself to the creed of the country, before he could have wielded or awakened the energies of the country. Accordingly, he began to blend high priests with the heroes of Thermopyle in his appeals to the national patriotism. In like manner, all our ungodly great men find it necessary to appear to have some religion, whenever they attempt to be philanthropic.

But, it may be said, are not all our great men, who are good men, embarked in the benevolent enterprises of the age. Some of them have written powerfully, others preached eloquently, and all subscribed on their behalf. Who, but them, originated and established our institutions! True. But ought it not to strike them with the force of a sensation, that, if their occasional efforts have been thus successful, their habitual efforts would have been glorious? If each of them had "lived, and moved, and had his being," in one of our institutions—throwing all his soul into it, and enthroning it wherever he went, and bending all things to its promotion, what would have been the effect? Upon themselves it would have been as dew upon the tender herb, both refreshing and invigorating. They would have had no time to watch their morbid symptoms, and no temptations to indulge melancholy. Who ever heard of an active philanthropist being "devoured by the vapors?" It is impossible to conceive of a Howard, a Wilberforce, or a Carey suffering from *ennui*, or sick of life. And, as to insanity, it seems physically, as well as morally impossible, in the case of minds absorbed with rational plans for the glory of God.

When mighty minds become mercy-seats to the world, like the ancient mercy-seat of the temple, they are guarded by cherubim, and enshrined by the divine presence. No cloud but "the cloud of glory," can settle upon them. At first sight, there may seem more fancy than fact in this assertion, and it is not true in the case of minds which have been shattered before they were consecrated to the good of mankind. These will, of course, be liable to interruptions of light and peace, however absorbed in their new object. But even such minds would gain, unspeakably, in composure and healthiness, by throwing themselves fully into a great object. No regimen of skill would so abate their unnatural action. It must be acknowledged, however, that both popular theory and supposed fact are against this opinion. The excitement, inseparable from public efforts, is held to be "a lion in the way." And, certainly, if habitual effort had the same effect as occasional, shattered minds might well shrink from publicity. There are also some kinds of publicity which highly susceptible minds ought to shrink from. But the ways in which great public objects may be promoted are as various as the objects themselves. They may be as effectually served in the parlor and in the study, as in the pulpit or on the platform. He who dare not speak, may write with safety. He who cannot move assemblies, without agitating himself, may inspire a succession of small circles. But the inactive are afraid of appearing ostentatious. Stepping forward to espouse a great cause, after having long shrunk from publicity, seems to imply a recognition of their own greatness if not to amount to a proclamation of it. There it is. They have not lost nor forgotten themselves in a great cause. Its bearing upon themselves is still the first question with them; a plain proof that they have not studied it sufficiently. The thing to be put forward is, not themselves, but the state of others, and the man who cannot both hide and forget himself in his exhibitions of a fallen world, has never fully sounded the depth of its fall, however great he may be in mind or morals.

Say not to yourself, "what has all this to do with me?" You have mind enough to make you miserable, if you live for yourself; because you live at a time when it is impossible to live ignorant of the wants and woes of a perishing world, or to pass unpunished for selfishness. The curse, even the bitter curse of Meroz, will find you out, wherever you skulk, if you come not to the "help of the Lord against the mighty." You must move on with the armies of the Living God to promote the glory of God, or be left in that sphere where neither grace nor Providence can be calculated on to work for your good. Say not, either, to yourself, "I cannot glorify God: nothing I am capable of doing could amount to such service." Let us examine this objection. Now, whilst it is certainly and emphatically condescension on the part of God to regard Himself as glorified by the works or the worship of the angelic hierarchy, still, it is obvious, that, if anything can glorify Him, their pure worship and perfect obedience must do so—because nothing finite can rise higher, or be holier, than the work and worship of angels. It is, therefore, not very difficult to conceive how God felt Himself to be really glorified, when these "morning stars" sang together over creation—and when they shouted Alleluia over the mysterious scenes of Providence—and when they sang a New Song on the completion of the majestic scheme of Redemption. For what more or better could they have done? They concentrated all their powers of observation upon these wonderful works of God, and celebrated them with all their powers of feeling and utterance. Accordingly, God condescended to accept of this adoring homage, just as they intended it—as the highest tribute of glory they could present. Even we ourselves feel, that, if we could burn with seraphic ardor, or bow with angelic humility, or serve with cherubic alacrity, that our worship would amount to something somewhat like glorifying God. It would, indeed, even then, be less than God deserves: but still, it would be immensely better than it is now, and more like a tribute of glory. As it is now, we find some difficulty in calling even our good works, obedience; or our best worship devotion. Even when we give most liberally to the cause of God, and suffer most patiently under the mighty hand of God, we hardly venture to say or think that we have glorified God. And were any one—however much a stranger to all flattery and compliment—to say to us, after the most signal act of obedience or submission—"Well, you have glorified God in this matter," we should feel afraid to say, "Yes," and even hesitate to say, "I hope so." Is this low estimate of what we do and give in the service of God, entirely from humility? Could no other cause be assigned for our modesty, than our conviction that, after having "done all," we are but unprofitable servants? Does not our shame arise oftenest from the consciousness of not having done all that we might have done for God?

However this may be, one thing is certain; that both in doing and giving in the service of God, we ought to aim expressly at glorifying God. He condescends to regard the service of men, as well as of angels, as a tribute of glory to Himself; and, therefore, it is neither humility nor good sense to shrink from viewing duty as God represents it. Why did not Paul say to the redeemed Corinthians, "Serve God with your body and spirit, seeing ye are bought with a price." Serving or obeying God includes all the acts and efforts which glorifying God includes: but still, Paul says, "Glorify God." Why? Obviously, because what is done with a view to honor or glorify God will be better done, even if there be no greater amount of obedience in the action itself. In general more will be done from this motive; because we are always more generous when we design to pay honor, than when we proceed to discharge debts. We apply the rule of bare justice to debts: but when we wish to honor a man, we do our utmost. So it is in the service of God. Until we are concerned both to please and glorify Him, we shall calculate how little will pass for service. But the moment we propose to ourselves to give God a mark of our love, or a pledge of our zeal, we shall try to do our best.

Let us inquire into the extent of the obligation to glorify God. Is it universally binding on all men, or is it binding only upon the redeemed? Now so far as the oracle, just quoted, is concerned, the duty is enforced only upon those who are "bought with a price," or redeemed by the precious blood of Christ. All such are emphatically "not their own;" but each of them under infinite obligations to glorify God. Are you, then, "your own," and under no such obligation? If you be not sure that you are redeemed by the blood of Christ, are you at liberty to employ your body and spirit, your time and talents, just as you like, so long as you do not, or cannot, regard yourselves as "the Redeemed of the Lord"? Does moral obligation not begin until personal redemption is ascertained, to our satisfaction, and sensibly enjoyed? If not—it is evident that there would be very few to enforce the obligation, to glorify God, upon. Yes: very few; for many of the avowed followers of Christ are afraid to say, "He loved me, and gave himself for me." Were, therefore, the duty to be confined to those who possess the assurance of faith; and were all free to live as they choose, who doubt their own redemption, how little could be done for the promotion of the divine glory at home or abroad! What ought I say on this subject? You see at a glance, that it might be rendered deeply and terribly controversial. It will not, however, be rendered so by me. I will confine myself to simple first principles, and keep you close to them, so long, at least, as you continue to read.

Now it is our interest to live to the glory of God, even if we knew nothing else about our personal redemption but just that we need to be redeemed. Men who need the redemption of their souls from sin and hell can only double their guilt and danger by neglecting to glorify God. Indeed, we could not do better, nor yet so well, as try to glorify Him, even if we did not need deliverance from the wrath to come. Were we, therefore, absolutely "our own," and thus irresponsible masters of our time and talents—of our powers and property—it would be our interest to consecrate ourselves, body, soul and spirit, unto God. For, mark these words — we must give ourselves up to something. Neither the soul nor the body can be kept out of all employment, or kept clear of all purposes. They will do something, and do it for the sake of some object. Money will go for something. Time will be well filled up in some way. Influence will forward some purpose. They cannot terminate entirely nor chiefly in themselves. We must have an object to live for, whatever it be. Now there is no object to be compared with the glory of God. What is done and given to promote that can neither be lost nor undone. It will tell on both the temporal and eternal benefit of mankind. It is as sure to do good as that God cannot lie. Accordingly, all that has been done for the glory of God in any age has done positive and permanent good to the world. In fact, more than one half of all our national privileges and social advantages spring, instrumentally, from what former generations did for the glory of God. Our remote ancestors did not, indeed, act on very pure principles, nor from the best of motives, when they filled the land with sanctuaries, and enriched it by seats of learning. There was much ostentation in their zeal, and more legality in their charities. They rather aimed at propitiating and bribing God than at glorifying Him. But still—what they spent in this way, God overruled for His own glory and thus for good to the country.

The matter comes, therefore, to this—What could we give ourselves to, that would be so good for ourselves or others, as the promotion of the divine glory? Are they gainers, in health or happiness, who do nothing for God? They act, indeed, as if they were their own; but they are the servants, if not the slaves, of something which often sickens them in this world, and never brightens the aspect of the next world. Even men of genius and talent (as we have seen) are invariably the victims of their own mighty powers whenever they live for their own fame, or for an object unworthy of eternity.

Let us, however, look at ourselves. Now we are not our own, whatever may be our relation to the redemption which is by Christ Jesus. Were we even excluded from it, or past redemption, we could not be absolutely our own. No man can be really independent of God. No man has any such possession of life, health, reason, or property, as to be sole master of them. He may refuse to glorify God with them; but he cannot resist God, if God lay His hand upon them. One man may look at the mystery of redemption and excuse himself; and another at its holiness and dislike it; and another at its claims and grudge them; but all three are equally at the disposal of God. They cannot take themselves out of His hands. It is, therefore, the very height of folly, as well as of effrontery, to evade the claims of God upon our time, property or power: for we have no time but just what He allows; no property but just what He spares; no powers but just what He sustains; and, therefore, we can only peril them all by devoting none of them to His glory. We are masters of nothing but of what He makes us masters; and of that, no longer or further than He thinks proper: and surely it is not the way to prolong possession to employ it contrary to the designs and demands of God. Whatever, therefore, be our real or imaginary position towards redemption now—this is our actual position towards all we are or have; entire and total dependence on the will of God.

It is not, therefore, redemption, that makes a man not his own. That increases and confirms his obligations to glorify God; but it does not create nor originate them. He could not be his own, even if there were no Redeemer; and as there is a Redeemer, able and willing to save unto the very uttermost, we ought willingly to consecrate ourselves to the divine glory. For it certainly will not, and cannot, hinder the redemption of any man to do whatever he can to glorify God. Is there no danger of falling into self-righteousness and self-dependence by trying to be good, and to do good, before conversion? May not a man rest in his doings and givings, and thus ruin his soul by overlooking the Savior? Alas! This is possible—for there is a natural and strong propensity in the heart to make a merit—even a righteousness, of well-doing and benevolence. There is, however, another side of the question low before us: will evil doing, or doing no good, forward a man's salvation, or prevent him from overlooking the Savior? No well-doing will or can merit salvation, certainly; but neither can the neglect of well-doing procure it, or tend to lead to it. Indeed, nothing can so peril the soul as sin and selfishness; because their direct tendency is to harden the heart, and to sear the conscience: and thus to send away and keep away the man from all the means of grace. Whereas, in doing something in the service and for the glory of God—the unconverted are brought and kept under the gospel; and thus exposed to the perpetual influence of a check upon their self-righteous and legal tendencies. That minister pays but a poor compliment to the gospel itself—and he tacitly passes a heavy reflection upon his own preaching of it who is afraid to urge upon the unconverted and undecided the duty of departing from evil and doing good. What is his preaching worth, if it cannot prevent such hearers from imagining that they are meriting grace or mercy? A minister ought to be as able to strip them of their own righteousness, as to stir them up to works of righteousness and charity. He ought as much to remember and teach that solemn oracle, which declares "he shall have judgment without mercy, who showed no mercy," as that which declares, that, "by the deeds of the law, no flesh living shall be justified."

Besides, trying to glorify God by good conduct and benevolence has a direct tendency to promote the redemption of the soul. We have seen that it cannot hinder salvation by grace, if the duty be wisely inculcated. How it can help it is also quite as obvious, when calmly considered. I mean, however, by help—nothing more than when I say that reading the scriptures and hearing the gospel help to promote the redemption of the soul. Now these are real helps towards acquiring the knowledge of the way of redemption—and knowledge of the need of redemption—and knowledge of the freeness, value, and holiness of it. Neither reading nor hearing help to ransom the soul —nor to pay its debts—nor to purchase its pardon—nor to merit heaven: but they do help to bring the soul acquainted with the worth of these blessings, and to bow the soul in humble prayer at the cross and the mercy-seat, for them. Now, just in the same way is trying to glorify God, a help. It merits nothing—it balances no account—it compensates for no sin; but it promotes the redemption of the soul, by promoting the knowledge of it, and concern for it. And in this way: let any man visit the death-bed of either a saint or a sinner to glorify God by manifesting sympathy, or by giving relief if it be wanted; and he will both hear and see, in the case of the former, how the hope of salvation can sustain patience under suffering, and impart composure even in the valley of the shadow of death: and, in the case of the latter, he will see either the anguish of remorse, or the insensibility of impenitence, which the neglect of the great salvation always produces. And will not this help to promote concern for his own salvation? Or, let him, from a regard to the glory of God, visit the Sunday school in his neighborhood, and mark, at once, both the patience of the teachers, and the varied manifestations of character in the children—and let the visits be repeated, and the progress of religion watched in this nursery for eternity; and he cannot fail to feel that ours is a world that needs redemption: and that man, even in childhood, is a creature naturally unfit for heaven, as well as unworthy of it. Or, let him consult the glory of God by considering the case of the perishing heathen—with whom he must be confronted at the judgment-seat—and for whom he could now do something by sending the gospel to them—and like whom, he would not be for worlds—and, will not this contrast of his own case with theirs, tend, and that mightily, to enhance the value of his privileges, and make him alive to his responsibility?

In a word, there is no department of zeal or benevolence but may prove instructive and impressive to any man; and thus useful to his soul. Consider now the peculiar force of the motive which personal redemption furnishes on behalf of living to the divine glory. *"Ye are not your own: you are bought with a price."* Paul does not say—a great price, nor an infinite price. He knew its greatness too well to attempt a description of it by words. In this he imitated the Savior, when he spoke of the love of God in providing a Redeemer. He did not say how much nor how warmly God loved the world: but with a simplicity which proves that description was baffled, he said, *"God so loved the world, as to give His only begotten Son."* In like manner, the precious blood of Christ is a ransom-price for the soul which cannot be reckoned. Like His love—"it passeth knowledge." Now, it was to this view of the redeeming price that the apostles and the primitive Christians adjusted the scale of their doing, giving, and suffering, for the glory of God and the Lamb. At Pentecost, no man but Ananias, said that "aught he had was his own." They even took joyfully the spoiling of their goods, and the loss of their lives. There, was the force of the motive.

The world never saw such a movement. It was, however, in fine harmony with all that had happened on the great day of atonement, when the price of redemption was paid. Then, the sun felt that its light was not its own—and shone not. The earth felt that its strength was not its own—and trembled. The dead felt that their graves were not their own—and came forth. Angels felt that their harps were not their own—and were silent. No wonder! The Lord of life and glory was not His own on that awful day. He was then *"the propitiation for our sins, and not for ours only, but also for the sins of the whole world."* He neither lived for Himself, nor died for Himself, whilst He was in our world; and both in living and dying, He left us an example, that we should walk in His steps. That example is as inspiring as it is perfect. Why, then, should the inspiration be lost on your heart, or its constraining influence uninfluential on your habits? You are not excluded from the benefits of his atoning sacrifice.

You are as welcome to trust in His cross, as you are obliged to copy His example. It is as much your duty to hope in Christ as to obey Christ. Let no man deceive you on this point. No man knows anything to the contrary, and you do not, cannot wish, to have neither part nor lot in the great propitiation. Whatever, therefore, you may have to suspect, or others insinuate, against your personal warrant and welcome to hope in Christ, neither you nor they can disprove your warrant or your welcome. Nothing could disprove either, but an express message from God, prohibiting hope. In your case: and even an angelic messenger would not be a sufficient voucher for the truth of such an interdict. You or I would, indeed, think it only too true, were "an angel (seemingly) from heaven" to announce it. We could never, perhaps get over such a discouragement: but still, the testimony of no single angel, unless accredited by as many and majestic miracles as the gospel presents, would warrant any man to believe that God had cut him finally off from mercy. And if there would be good reason to suspect, that an apparent seraph, with such a message, was but "Satan transformed into an angel of light," what is the worth or weight of any man's speculations, or of your own suspicions, about your personal welcome? Nothing can disprove or discredit it, whilst God continues you under the gospel. It would, indeed, be ominous, if you were struck blind, like Simon, for your past treatment of the good ways of God: but even in that case, apostolic counsel would be, "repent of thy wickedness, and pray God, if perhaps the thought of thine heart may be forgiven thee."

In a word, you have to do with nothing but the gospel, so far as the question of your own warrant to hope for salvation is concerned. Neither man nor angel can invalidate the invitation, or the command which it presses upon you. Take care, therefore, that you yourself neither adopt nor give way to any opinion or surmising which tends to make the gospel not "good news" to you. No matter what such a suspicion is drawn from nor in what spirit it is indulged; it impugns the grace of the gospel just as infidelity impugns the truth of the gospel. There is, indeed, a mighty difference between the man who suspects that he has no part nor lot in the great redemption, and the man who denies the truth of redemption. The latter is both a sceptic and a scorner: whereas the former may have no ill will nor bad design against the gospel. Nothing, therefore, can be farther from my intention, than to identify the two. Still, if a man so strip the gospel of its grace that he can only "tremble" whilst he believes; he is, however unintentionally, impugning its character. It was not sent to make him tremble of sorrow, as one for whom there is no hope. It is as much glad tidings as it is true tidings: and, therefore, if he would shrink with horror from raking up the ashes of heresy and controversy, to make out a pretense against its truth, he ought not to rake up either the ashes of his old sins, nor the plagues of his own heart, to find reasons for doubting its grace. Any heart or life would, indeed, furnish overwhelming proof that there is an utter unworthiness of grace, and no possibility of meriting it. Salvation is, however, graciously promised in answer to prayer, and that by a God who cannot lie; and, therefore, it is just as wrong to doubt of success, as it would be to demand legally.

It is not, however, here, that you are in most danger. The kind of doubts to which the last paragraph refers, are not very likely to cross your mind, except when you want an excuse for living unto yourself, or for neglecting to glorify God in your body and spirit. Most solemnly, therefore, do I warn and abjure you not to tamper with the questions which are kept afloat about the extent of redemption. At your peril take nothing from that quarter to excuse yourself from activity or benevolence in the cause of God. Your body and spirit are His, however you may speculate about "secret things." Your all is in His hands, at His disposal—at His will: you, therefore, risk everything if you do nothing to glorify God. And in your case, temporal ruin, or the more tremendous curse of a portion in this life only, must be the consequence of sloth and selfishness; because you have little or no temptation to doubt, except for worldly purposes.

An ignorant or weak man may stand idle amidst the activities of the church from sheer inability to comprehend the connection between diligence and dependence, means and ends; but you can plead no such excuse. Bring together now the hints thrown out in this essay. Let both the warnings and the wooings commend disinterested public spirit to your heart and conscience. Resolve not to live unloved, nor to die unmissed. Never think of going to heaven alone; except when you want to be stirred up to try how many you can take with you. Make sure of one, and you will be sure to try to win more. Let not these claims upon your co-operation surprise you. You can co-operate in promoting the divine glory. Had you no other talent but the power of teaching children to read in the Sunday school; and no other time but the intervals of public worship—you may be a great blessing in your neighborhood. And whatever be your talents, this would not be unworthy of a part of your time. That young man's mental vision is either weak or jaundiced, who sees no glory about Sunday schools. True; they are not "the sun that rules by day, nor the moon that rules by night," in the moral world; but they are the stars of its firmament, created and sustained by the same hand that planted the sanctuary and pointed to the closet. They are too, stars that will fight "in their courses," against the Siseras of tyranny, and superstition, and infidelity. He who "bringeth out the hosts of heaven in their seasons," brought out these schools, in the season when the history of the world was about to begin anew, and when the institutions of the world began to be remodeled. Rational liberty wanted them. The age of Bibles wanted them. Missionary enterprise wanted them. Slavery could not have been abolished without them. They have "greatly helped" on all that is good or promising at home and abroad. Not that they taught children the elements of wise policy, or of public spirit: but the men who taught children and saw children learn to read the Bible saw also what a nation reading the Bible should be and would be. Philanthropists learned more than they intended to teach. Even mere politicians, although they knew not how it was created, found a public opinion abroad in the country upon which every moral question could fall back without losing ground, and rest until it was irresistible.

For, why can no great moral question be lost now? Obviously, because its merits can be appreciated at once by all the friends of education. And they see them, not only in the abstract, but also in their practical bearings upon a Bible-taught community. Thus whilst there are no politics in Sunday schools, they help mightily to place and keep all national objects in their true light. But the grand bearings of these seminaries are upon eternity. This is not seen, however, when attention is confined to the instances of early piety, which individual schools present to the eye. These are not few: but they are nothing, to the general preparation which is made for eventual piety. There is something for the gospel to work upon—to appeal unto—in all who learn to read the word of God. They can never forget all their lessons, nor lose all their early impressions. Both prosperity and adversity will recall the memory of their teachers, their class, and their convictions of duty; and thus Providence, as well as Grace, will find much to turn into account. And they will turn it to good account. This sowing "to the Spirit," is itself, a pledge that Providence will watch, and the Spirit water, the seed of eternal life. God would never have put it into the hearts of so many to sow the precious seeds in the hearts of the young, had He not intended to produce an eventful harvest of ripe fruits, which should bless the earth, and even beautify the heaven of heavens. Consecrated teachers will, therefore, see, long before the day of judgment declare it, that they had not labored in vain. They will often hear the harps of angels struck to celebrate the repentance of some of their scholars. Their mansions of glory will be frequently gladdened by the entrance of some to whose childhood they ministered on earth, and in whose maturity and fellowship they shall rejoice forever. Be a teacher, if you can do nothing else. There will be a "Sunday-School Jubilee" in heaven, as surely as there will be a ministerial jubilee.

But you can do more than teach children: you can learn "to speak a word in season," to the sick and the dying. Amongst them too, a harvest may be reaped which shall sweeten your own life and swell the songs of eternity. The lingering death-beds of the poor and the wretched are the last appeals which God makes to our sympathies on behalf of their souls. It is not by accident that they suffer so much or so long. He is giving them "space for repentance," that we may give them the knowledge of salvation. He forbears to cut them down at once, as cumberers of the ground, that we dig about them, and thus see if they will bear fruit. Work, therefore, for God, if you would not weep, in time.

6

Of Manly Estimates of the Evil of Sin

It is just as true that trifles are not sins, as that sins are not trifles. Whist, therefore he is emphatically a fool who "mocks at sin," he is certainly not a wise man who reckons everything sinful, which some good people call so. There are singular consciences amongst the pious, as well as "seared consciences" amongst the profane. Better, indeed, "strain" equally at a gnat and a camel, than "swallow" both at once, or either with equal ease. Singularity is infinitely better, as well as safer, than insensibility; but, as both are extremes, they ought to be carefully avoided: the former, that our "good may not be evil spoken of;" and the latter, that we may not make "shipwreck of a good conscience." It has long been proverbial—and long may it continue so—that singularity is the safest side to err on: but still, an error in judgment, even as in favor of piety, is not a desirable auxiliary to piety. It furnishes those who dislike religion with a pretense against religion. You have heard of the "pious frauds" of Popery. This name is given to the first series of false miracles and visions which were got up in favor of religion, before the Romish Church traded in "lying wonders" and popular delusion. And although, of course, no fraud can be pious, it is not improbable that some good men really meant well when they connived at the pretense— of holy relics, and heavenly visions, and miraculous images. At least, they did not intend to furnish infidelity with weapons against revelation; nor anticipate that the scorners of future ages would confound Christianity itself with the superstitions of that age. Good intentions did not, however, prevent bad consequences. The school of Voltaire and Volney unmasked these frauds, and impudently charged them upon Christianity, although it had both predicted and denounced them as "lying wonders." In like manner, there is no small danger of thinking too lightly of sin itself, when trifles are held up as sinful, or singularities paraded as virtuous. Sin is the transgression of the laws of God, and the penalty of sin is the wrath of God: things, infinitely too solemn to be enforced against trifles, or matters of doubtful disputation. We ought, therefore, to be very careful to confine the epithet sinful to the actions and dispositions which God calls sinful; and never to confound real infirmities, or mere accidents, with sins. For, when everything that is not strictly religious is reckoned sinful, what is really sinful will not be reckoned very criminal or dangerous.

It is not—Oh, it is not by confessing that "in all things we sin," that we shall acquire the deepest hatred or fear of sin. Such a confession looks humble, and may be well meant; but it is anything but holy in its influence, except on those who are far advanced in holiness. Upon the generality, it has just this effect; they regard sinning as so much a matter of course, that they are afraid of nothing but flagrant crimes. Accordingly, if they keep clear of them, they make no great effort to be very circumspect; for having laid their account with sinning in all things, they excel in nothing. Because they can do nothing perfectly, they do not try how well anything can be done. Because "we deceive ourselves" if we say we have "no sin," they do not exert themselves to avoid sin, nor to discover how little it may be reduced to. Because they confess it in all things, they imagine that they cannot forsake it entirely in anything. *"This is a sore evil under the sun."* Should these hints commend themselves to your common sense, you must not be surprised if some people both question their truth, and express alarm at their tendency. Eminently good people will, indeed, be glad to see you discriminate between weakness and wickedness, infirmity and sin: but those who have not conscience enough to try how well they can act, will, in order to hush up their suspicions of themselves, suspect you of some doctrinal heresy. Let no clamor tempt you, however, to confound trifles with sins. If you come to do that, you will soon confound sins with trifles, and take both easily. Better try how much truth you can speak, than have to confess lies, however humbly. Better try how temperate you can be every day, than have to weep over excess, however penitently. Better try how much you can govern your tongue and temper, than have to stand self-condemned for the neglect of self-control. Those who deem it enough to ask pardon for such sins, without guarding against the recurrence of them, may insinuate, that you are too proud to feel your need of daily pardon; and too ignorant of the spirituality of the divine law to be aware of your sinfulness. All this is easily said; and you ought to retort it solemnly, whenever it is said by those who blunder through life without much rule or conscience. You have, indeed, much to learn, both in regard to the extent of the divine requirements and your need of daily pardon: but you will not learn either well by leaving truth, temperance, or self-control, to accident and circumstances. In fact, nothing could blind you more to the spirituality of the eternal law, than falling into the habit of regarding it as a matter of course, that sinning in all things is inevitable. Imperfection in all things is inevitable: but there is a mighty difference between coming short of the standard, after an honest effort to do well, and the sin of making no effort, or the sloth of letting duty take its chance. Try, therefore, to do your very best in something good, if you would ascertain either your own weakness, or your absolute need of mercy and grace.

On the other hand, great care must be taken, lest the real distinctions between sin and imperfection, fault and foible, be perverted. "A straw will show which way the wind blows;" and things, in themselves, but trifling, reveal the real state of the heart. It is, therefore, no answer to a charge of ungodliness, when it happens to be made in connection with the animated pursuit of some amusement, to ask—"What harm is there in that amusement?" This is an unmanly subterfuge, if the pursuit engross all your spare time and absorb all your thoughts. Then—it is no trifle, for it has banished God from the mind, outweighed eternity, and infatuated the soul. It is very easy to get up special pleadings on behalf of a favorite object, and to prove that there is nothing in its nature or tendency, which is morally wrong: but the real question is—what place does it occupy in your heart, and what portion of your time does it consume? Music is not sinful, nor painting a waste of time, nor science unworthy of a Christian; but if they usurp the throne of the heart, what more could the worst vice do? It is the heart that God claims; and if it be withheld from Him, a literary excuse will avail as little as a sensual or secular apology. How could it be otherwise? It is, indeed, right to improve the mind by literature, and not wrong to blend some amusement with study: but it is an utter perversion of terms—an outrage on common sense and decency—to call that an improvement of the mind which banishes God from the mind: to call that an amusement, which renders divine and eternal things unpleasant to the heart.

How language can be abused! "I am only improving my mind;" said a young man who was leaving neither time nor thought for religion. Science and literature were his all in all. He confessed that he never prayed—seldom opened the Bible—and never enjoyed the sanctuary: and yet, he pretended that he was improving his mind! I need not, surely, expose either the fallacy or the effrontery of this pretense. He might just as well have talked of the morning star improving its brilliancy by receding from the sun. He certainly forgot that the eternal improvement of the mind will arise from eternal contemplation of divine things. How then can that be a step towards it, which is a departure from them? But, I forbear.

Harmless and even proper objects, may be pursued in a spirit and to a degree which render them as fatal to the soul as flagrant crimes can be. Is it not, then, of immense, yea, of infinite importance, to form solid and solemn views of the evil of sin? It should be as impossible for us to think lightly of any sin, as of the shrieks of bodily agony, or the yells of mental disease. It should be held as infamous and unnatural to smile at sin, as to mock at suffering: for "sin is the transgression of the law." If this consideration does not make you tremble at sin, you must have very vague notions of the eternal law. Did you ever look at the exact amount of your knowledge of divine law? Did you ever question yourself on the subject? True, the law is the rule of life to us; but it as much so as if an angel walked at our side, pointing out the path of duty and waving a flaming sword against every sin. It is more! It is such a rule of life as if we heard the actual voice of Jehovah behind us, saying, *"This is the way, walk ye in it, and turn neither to the right hand nor the left."* Yea, were the King Eternal visible, we could not be more obligated to dread sin than we now are, however much more awed we might be.

We are, indeed, very much the creatures of circumstances; and, accordingly, were Sinai to thunder again from time to time, or its lightnings again to lighten the world, the law would command attention. But, what are thunders however loud, or lightnings however vivid, compared with the calm majesty of Jehovah's solemn silence? In that deep calm, we hear the beatings of His heart against sin; and yet all in sympathy towards sinners. God is too much in earnest to thunder law, now that man can read it—and now that nations do not require forty years' discipline in a wilderness before they can discern between good and evil. Having finished redemption from the curse of the law by the atonement of His Son, God has finished, too, the process of enforcing obedience by miracles; and thrown man, in the manhood of the world, upon the mighty energies and resources of the new covenant; that thus conscience might be the Sinai of the law, and memory and judgment its tables, and the heart its ark. Thus God treats us as men, that we may be manly in our venerations of divine law. It is to the moral universe, what the laws of nature are to the material universe—the source and the secret of strength and order. Who would tamper with the law of gravitation in the solar system, or try to stop the smallest wheel in the machinery of that system, even if he could disturb them? The bare idea of falling stars and loosened comets would paralyze the boldest hand; or an indignant world would arrest and chain it. He is, however, a greater enemy of his species, and of his own soul, who would destroy or disturb the authority of moral law, as a whole, or in any of its parts.

It will also help you to form solid and solemn views of the evil of sin, if you will calculate the tendency of any sin to prolong and spread itself. It does not stop when the sinner stops, nor die at his death.

"The guilty ambition of Jeroboam put into operation a principle of evil which gathered strength and malignant energy by the lapse of ages, and gave rise to a complication of crime, and a continued accumulation of suffering, which omniscience alone can fully estimate or understand."— Dr. Gordon

This awful case, although singular in degree, is not so in kind. Even in degree, Voltaire was the Jeroboam of France. The leaven of infidelity, which he infused into the lump of continental society, has not, indeed, "leavened the whole lump:" but how widely it has wrought—how deeply it has penetrated—how direfully it has operated! And, when is it likely to work itself out, or be eradicated?

It is not, indeed, so easy to trace the trail of the seducer, a gambler, a forger, or a drunkard, throughout all the circle and cycle of his influence: but each of them also transmits to posterity the venom of his own besetting sin. Their immediate victims are not their only, perhaps not their chief victims. The immediate victim of a seducer is a daughter of parents whose hearts are well-nigh broken by her fall: the sister of brothers or sisters whose place and prospects in life are lowered by her fall: the mother of a child who inherits shame, and has no fair chance of acquiring character. Thus the evil begins to ramify. And all this is but the beginning of sorrows and sin. Her brothers and sisters, thrown into a lower sphere of life, with less self-respect, and fewer friends, continue to sink in the scale of society; and, then, their offspring, like her own, rise up to spread and perpetuate misery and crime. The seducer originates this incalculable and interminable line of evil! Employ it, therefore, to fathom his depth in guilt.

The fraud and forgery of extravagance work in the same way. The guilt of the Lothario is not measured, nor its results calculated, when the money he has squandered is summed up, nor when the feelings of his family are reckoned. More than the hopes of his parents are blasted. Their place in society is altered, however much they retain the sympathy of society. They cannot place another of their sons, however steady, in the confidential situation which their prodigal abused. Even their daughters, however deserving, are thrown from the vantage ground of commanding influence. Not, indeed, that either the sisters or brothers of the prodigal are at all identified with him in principle or character, nor at all suspected: but still, they have not all their wonted influence. They cannot do nor attempt all they once could. Even when others can forget or overlook the cloud which has fallen on their house, the family themselves cannot. They are unable to breathe under it with their usual freedom; or to walk beneath it, with all the natural independence of their original bearing. They do not exactly stoop, nor succumb, nor shrink, nor falter: but yet, they are not altogether their former selves. Thus the fraudulent spendthrift breaks the heart of his parents, and cripples the energies of the whole family. And, what is he himself, wherever he may go? True, he may retrieve his character abroad. There are solitary instances of successful reformation amongst both voluntary and transported exiles. But whatever else they gain or regain, they never recover self-respect. When that morning star of the breast has set amidst the tear and shame of home, it never rises again in another hemisphere, however character may rally, or property accumulate. Even piety cannot restore lost self-respect. It is not intended to do so. It is one of its glories, that it deepens self-condemnation, in the very proportion that it relieves the heart from the fear of final condemnation. Wherever, therefore, such an exile is —whether amidst the sunny plains of Australia, or the solemn forests of America—every attempt he makes to render the wilderness a fruitful field, and especially its success, when "the wilderness blossoms like the rose," forces back his thoughts to his father-land and entangles them with all the painful associations of home. For he cannot help assimilating his foreign house, and garden and fields, to the home-model; and thus, as they advance to perfection, they throw him back at every step upon the scenes of his youth. He cannot forget, whatever be his character: and if he is indeed, "a new man," he never can forgive himself, however vivid or strong his hopes of divine forgiveness may be. Self-condemnation will be a perpetual and ponderous balance-wheel upon all his hopes and joys. He may marry well, and be justly beloved both as a husband and a father; but he has a secret which he dare not confide to the wife of his bosom; and he must tell his children a garbled tale, when they ask him about his country parents; and he may acquire and deserve the esteem of his neighbors; but even that, when it is most gratifying, will awaken "the gnawing worm" of his deep consciousness —that if they knew all they would not respect him. He may even take a commanding place in civil and religious society, and become as useful as he is reformed; but no public confidence nor private deference, he may receive, can ever restore the early sunshine of his conscience. It is impossible, in the very nature of things. The millstone he hung around his own neck, at home, he must carry with him wherever he goes; and even if no one see it or suspect it, it will often sink his spirits in a sea of agony or abstraction, which he cannot entirely conceal from others.

It is necessary to speak out on this painful subject. I would not take from any parent or his prodigal anything that the proverb—"many a broken ship has come to land"— really teaches. Such a broken ship, however, can no more sail on trading voyages in her old seas: and in new seas she must sail water-logged, however well she may be repaired or piloted. These hints on the evil of sin are additional to those in the first part of this series of Guides; and should not be judged of, apart from the arguments, there, founded on the character of God, and the cross of Christ.

7

Paul's Manly Glorying in the Cross

"God forbid that I should glory save in the Cross."

God forbid! Paul states. Why, God has forbidden all glorying which is not in Christ crucified. Accordingly, the express and authoritative command of God is, *"He that glorieth, let him glory in the Lord."* Glorying in anything but His cross is solemnly forbidden by the voice of all the sacrifices. From the altar of Abel to the last altar in the second temple, their united voice is, *"Without the shedding of blood there is no remission of sins."* It is forbidden by all the harps of prophecy: they mingle their sweet notes around the cross of Emmanuel, and the swell of their harmonious chorus is, *"Neither is there salvation in any other."* It is forbidden by all the trumpets of the gospel: their uniform and re-echoing peal is *"Christ is all and all."* It is forbidden by all the armies of heaven. Cherubim and seraphim forbid it, by their adoration of the Lamb slain. Angels and archangels forbid it, by their admiration of the sufferings. The noble army of martyrs and the general assembly of the redeemed forbid it, by their universal and eternal song. *"Unto him that loved us and washed us in his own blood, be glory forever."* Nothing—no sin, in the whole catalogue of crime, is so often, so loudly, so solemnly, forbidden, as glorying in anything save the cross of Christ. Paul knew all this well; far better than I can express or conceive; and yet he felt it necessary to pray, in the face of all these facts; *"God forbid that I should glory save in the cross."* Why? The apostle was afraid of his own heart; and therefore felt anxious, that what God had spoken by His word, should be re-spoken by his Spirit; and thus all legal glorifying be effectually forbidden in his mind forever.

And is not such an inward forbidding wanted in your soul? The outward prohibition has sounded in your ears like the Sinai trumpet, long and loud; but how few glory at all in the cross—how many glory in anything rather than the cross. Oh! There is need for prayer, and reflection too, that this neglect and coldness toward Christ crucified may be overcome and remedied. But this it never will be, by the formal and passing "God forbid" of the slothful or thoughtless. Neglect will, however, prove their ruin, if they do not procure its ruin; and kill the soul, if not killed in the soul.

Consider this, ye that forget God. The language of Paul is not, however, chiefly that of prayer: it is a burning burst of holy indignation against false teachers and false doctrine. Paul had sown the Galatian field with "good seed," and the enemies of the cross had come after him sowing tares. He had formed a church around the cross; and for a time it was united, steadfast, and holy. Its standard was its strength. Satan knew this, and turned his strength against the cross. Reproach opened all her mouths to defame it; persecution wielded all her weapons to defeat it; philosophy branded it as foolishness; legality gnashed her teeth at it, in mingled rage and contempt; until in Galatia it was held disgraceful and found to be dangerous to glory in the cross of Christ. Then its summer friends, like swallows, fled from the winter of its unpopularity. Its avowed enemies erected a new standard formed out of the wrecks of Judaism; and, by compulsion or fraud, were gathering a new church around it. Paul saw this melancholy defection and wept; saying, *"O foolish Galatians, who hath bewitched you, that ye should not obey the truth, before whose eyes Jesus Christ hath been evidently set forth crucified."* Paul saw this shameful defection, and kindled as the ancient prophets were wont, when they beheld the rival altars of Baal and Moloch: *"If any man,"* said he, *"preach any other gospel, let him be accursed."* The conscientious apostle looked upon the ministers of this heresy, and seeing them truckling to the public taste; entangling the weary and terrifying the weak—he despised their baseness; and, feeling himself crucified to the world, which enslaved them, exclaimed, *"God forbid that I should glory save in the cross."* The holy and happy apostle looked also upon the wandering sheep of his scattered fold: the dew of heaven was no longer on their fleece; Mount Zion no longer yielded green pastures, nor the river of life still waters for them; the Sun of Righteousness ceased to shine upon their souls, and the joy of the Holy Ghost was withdrawn from their hearts. They had forsaken the cross for another standard; and the consolations which are in Christ forsook them. Paul saw this; and pitying them, and feeling all his own happiness unimpaired, exclaimed, *"God forbid that I should glory save in the cross"*

Thus, too, I look around upon the ministers ashamed of the cross, and the ministers who deride it; and seeing the former afraid of the world's dread laugh, and the latter not afraid to mangle the word of God, I, too, adopt the apostolic maxim. And when I see the heartlessness and unhappiness, the suspense and uncertainty, and finally the hopeless death of those who do not glory in the cross—I must pray and cry, *"God forbid that I should glory save in the cross."* These general hints will prepare us for a more minute and spirited examination of this apostolic maxim. Consider it as the sentiment of Paul himself: *"God forbid that I."* What are you? Paul was too humble to publish his whole character, except as a sinner. But remember that he was as a man of talent and strong common sense. His grasp of intellect, and solidity of judgment, give weight to all his fixed sentiments, and especially to the one grand sentiment in which he gloried. He had not only examined the doctrine of the cross; but was able to examine it with a discriminating eye, and a calm judgment. He threw all his mighty mind into the question of salvation; and this was the result of his profound deliberations, *"God forbid that I should glory save in the cross."* Now, if on a question of astronomy, it would show no wisdom to differ in opinion with Newton; nor with Milton, on poetry; nor with Raphael, on painting—it cannot be creditable to any understanding to differ from Paul on the way of salvation. No man can think him weak or credulous. If therefore, great names should have great weight, Paul's is as great as it is good. There is not a greater in the ample roll of immortal fame. And then he is not alone in thus glorying only in the cross. He himself, I have no doubt felt the weight of the names which preceded his own, in this preference of Christ. It is perfectly in harmony with the character of his mind, to suppose, that the memory of the venerable patriarchs and holy prophets influenced him, in adopting this maxim. As if he had said,

"God forbid that I should glory save in the cross: Abraham, in all the majestic calmness of his character, did so: Moses in all the vigor of his intellect, did so: Elijah in all the glow of his energy, did so: David, in all the loveliness of his genius, did so: Isaiah in all the loftiness of his eloquence, did so: Job in all the integrity of his heart, did so: John the Baptist in all the stern simplicity of his character, did so: and shall I, Saul of Tarsus, not do the same? Compassed about, as I am, with so great a cloud; witnesses who all glorified in the promised Savior, just as he was promised as "the Lamb slain," can I do less? No, indeed; in Him all the patriarchs gloried; in him all the holy prophets. I am not alone on Mount Calvary. The mountain is covered with horses and chariots of fire; and above it, cherubim bend from their thrones of light, archangels sweep their harps of gold; all glorying in the same Savior. "God forbid that I should glory save in the cross of our Lord Jesus Christ."

And, do you say, amen, and amen? Do you hesitate? The hesitation is neither creditable to your taste nor judgment. And yet you wish, yea hope, to sit down in the kingdom of heaven, through eternity, with these mighty patriarchs, and with all the just men made perfect! You never will, if you sit not down with them under the cross, glorying in it as the only refuge of your soul. I congratulate all who have done so;

in coming to Jesus the Mediator of the new covenant, and to the blood of sprinkling, they are come to an innumerable company of angels, and to the general assembly and church of the firstborn, whose names are written in heaven. Remember Paul's learning as well as his talents. A powerful intellect, when not disciplined by education, and regulated by general knowledge, is often rash and singular in its habits; inquiring where it should reason, and reasoning where it should adore. But Paul was as well educated, as he was highly gifted. He examined the doctrine of the cross with a mind equally cultivated and powerful. His choice, is not, therefore, liable to suspicion, as the eccentricity of a bold genius or the dazzling vision of a daring imagination. What he admired, he had examined; what he adored, he had scrutinized; what he gloried in, he had weighed in all the balances of Scripture and sound learning. With Jewish law he had been familiar from his infancy; and with Gentile philosophy his acquaintance was intimate. He was therefore qualified to judge of the agreement of the doctrine of the cross, with the whole scope of Judaism and the entire principles of right reason. And the result of this learned process was the settled conviction—the sublime resolution—to glory only in the cross. I place that fact in this point of view, that the scholar may have no literary excuse for hesitating to imitate Paul; nor the unlearned be afraid to confide in his judgment. All are safe, and all act rationally, to abide by the apostle's verdict, on the question of salvation. Remember also his holy regard to pure morals. This gives immense weight to his glorying in the cross. Men have sought refuge under it for sin, and turned the grace of God into licentiousness—and thus proved that there is a kind of glorying even in the cross which "is not good." But it was not to indulge sin, nor to avoid self-denial, that Paul was the champion of the cross: he gloried in it, because by its influence he was crucified to the world, and the world crucified to him. He clung to it that he might excel and persevere in all personal and relative virtues; and whoever took a different view of its practical design, he denounced as *"enemies of the cross, whose glory was their shame, and their end destruction."*

If, therefore, misled, at all, by legal clamor, or legal caution, you are afraid of such glorying as I contend for, I triumphantly answer that the greatest champion of the cross was at once the greatest champion and example of morals the world ever saw (Christ excepted), from the day he began to glory only in the cross, until the moment that he died for it. I challenge even his enemies to prove, from one act of his apostolic life, that his glorying was not good. You perceive that my object is to commend and enforce the example of Paul; and therefore I will remind you that his glorying only in the cross was highly consistent with his views of himself as a sinner. He was now a saint, but he never forgot what he had been. The wormwood and gall of his natural state—his soul had still in remembrance, and was humbled within him. No wonder He had been the chief of sinners: and, having found mercy through the cross—might well glory only in it. Nowhere else could Saul of Tarsus have found refuge for his guilty soul. Methinks, the mercy seat of his own temple would have shrunk from his approach; the cloud of glory shot out avenging lightnings, and the cherubim flapped their wings to spurn the blaspheming persecutor. Paul felt more than this: that even the eternal mercy seat of the heavens must have spurned him, had it not been sprinkled by the blood of atonement. Well, therefore, might he glory in that cross which furnished the blood, which was set at once his ransom and his plea. Besides, he knew (and let the best of your class remember it) that Abraham with all his faith, Moses with all his meekness, Job with all his patience, David with all his devotion, Isaiah with all his holiness—that all the holy men of old required to glory only in the cross for their salvation. And, could he do less: Can you be saved in any other way than such men needed? If they all washed their robes and made them white in the blood of the Lamb, what else can cleanse you or me?

Come, let us realize, until we surround ourselves with the just men made perfect. Look at the glorious throng around the throne. Some of them were once worse than us. But oh! How many were much better! Better than we can pretend to be. Well, the best of them all, the brightest stars in that firmament of glory, owe all their salvation to the cross of Christ. How then can you escape if you neglect or do not glory in that cross? His glorying only in the cross was highly consistent with his views of himself as a child of God, and as a minister of the gospel. He did not cease to glory in the cross when he became an heir of eternal glory. Nay, he did not glory in it less when at the height of his holiness than he did at the beginning of it; but his glorying in the cross kept pace with the rapid progress of his sanctification, and kindled into new ardor as he advanced in meekness in heaven. The fact is worthy of profound attention.

Paul was now safe for eternity, and knew that he was safe. The settled persuasion of his mind was, that *"neither things present, nor things to come, could separate him from the love of God."* Both his calling and election were sure to himself. He had no more doubt of his being a child of God than of his existence as a man. Now, how did this full assurance operate upon his mind and character? We see many far less holy or happy, who decline in that glorying in the cross with which they began their profession of faith. Having obtained some hope of salvation, and some shadow of sanctification from the blood of atonement, they seem, if not to forget the cross, to feel less indebted to it; and less dependent on it. There is about some, an evident falling off from the devout, adoring, and lively interest, which marked their fast clinging to this tree of life: and as their fears of perishing have lessened, their attachment to it, has languished. Now to such, and to you, I point out the fact that it was not so in the case of Paul. His sense—his assurance—of final safety neither finished nor diminished his glorying in the cross; but the habit grew with the growth of his piety, and strengthened with the strength of his assurance. Familiarity with the cross, and happiness from it, had the same effect on his mind, as forever singing the new song in heaven will have on the minds of the glorified—the effect of endearing it more and more, and of keeping it forever new.

And, be it known, that this was not a needless nor an uncalled-for glorying in the cross, now that Paul was safe for eternity. You mistake the matter widely, if you imagine that his Sonship left it optional or indifferent whether he grew or declined in this habit: for, Paul owed it to himself to persist in glorying only in the cross. He was now indeed a saint; but he was not perfect. The law of God was indelibly engraved on his mind; but the law of sin was still in his members. He was crucified to the world, and the world crucified to him; but, in the emphatic language of Christ, he was still *"in the world,"* and needed to be kept from the evil of it. And, although, his attainments in piety were great, he counted not himself to have attained; but, forgetting the things behind, reached forward to things before him, that he might apprehend that for which he was apprehended by God. He could not, therefore, afford to cease or slacken his first glorying in the cross. Perfection of heart and character was now his supreme object; his grand pursuit: nothing else would satisfy him; and, as nothing but the cross could secure it, in nothing else would he glory; and in that, nothing less than when his piety was in its infancy. But he also owed it to others as well as to himself to persist in this habit His heart was set upon winning and keeping souls to Christ; and, therefore, in both cases, it was equally his duty to glory only in the cross. For this, in the case of those who were won, was the best check he could put on their tendency to declension.

Now we have seen that there is a sad tendency to decline from "first love," even where that love is genuine; and a disposition to argue from some growth in grace, as if we could do with less attention to the cross than we began with. But, here, we are met by Paul the aged; in the very beauty of holiness, in the maturity of his experience, at the height of his piety; and he—he at this stage —he in this state, cannot do, tries not to do, with any less clinging to Christ crucified, than when he first laid hold on Him for eternal life. Now, if he was right in acting thus —we are wrong whenever we relax our hold of the cross, or try the experiment of living less by faith on the Son of God. Oh, let the example of "Paul the aged," shame us, who believe out of sloth, and charm us into the habit of hanging as it were daily on the Savior's cross; breathing the Savior's prayer—*"Father, unto thy hands, I commend my spirit."*

But the apostle's example has an equally important bearing upon the case of those who are awakened but not won to Christ. Such, seeing nothing good about themselves, and much that is truly excellent about some true believers, imagine that until they attain some goodness they cannot be welcome to believe on the Savior for themselves. Their prevailing assurance is that while their hearts are so bad as they feel them to be, they have no right nor warrant to hope in Christ's salvation; and, that it is owing to something good about believers, that they are able and warranted to hope as they do. Hence the frequent expression, addressed by such to the pious—"Were I as good as you are, I might venture to hope and to take comfort from the promises, but while I am what I am, I dare not venture." Now it ought to be a sufficient answer to this false reasoning, that every godly man will say at once, "If there be any thing good about me now, it all began when I began to hope in Christ for salvation. It is all the effect of believing; and in nowise the cause of my faith. And even now, I feel more deeply than at first, that there is nothing between me and hell but just the blood of the Lamb. I am as much if not more than ever, bound to believe entirely, or despairing entirely." This, I say, should be a satisfactory answer to all the objections which awakened sinners start and strain against themselves; but if this will not suffice, here is a living lecture on the subject—Paul, the improved, the holy, the laborious, glorying only in the cross. Yes; when he was the wonder of the world for piety, and the most majestic pillar of the church for everything great and good, even then, he saw nothing between him and hell but glorying in the cross alone. It was all his salvation and all his desire. Every hope he cherished was founded on the blood of atonement; and every grace of his character was acquired by faith in it. He saw nothing, thought of nothing, depended on nothing, in or about himself; but clung to the cross as simply as the dying thief. What a lesson to all, and especially to those who are afraid to trust their naked souls to the finished work of Christ. And be it known to you, that in all this silence about everything but the cross, Paul was not carrying his self-denial or humility to an extreme. His conduct was humble, compared with that of many: but he did, he felt, nothing more than is necessary, when he thus fully put and kept out of sight everything but his faith in Christ. He was silent on nothing that deserved to be mentioned: for nothing deserves mentioning but the cross of Christ, when the salvation of the soul is spoken of. Indeed, everything we admire about the apostle was part of that salvation and the effect of glorying in the cross; and, therefore, could be no cause of either. Paul, therefore, owed it to others to exemplify this fact by his own spirit and habits. But he owed it likewise to God and the Lamb—to continue glorying only in the cross.

The Savior never tires of appearing in the midst of the throne as a Lamb that has been slain; nor does God cease to be well pleased with the atonement of His Son; nor does the Eternal Spirit weary in glorifying Christ; and therefore, both as a minister and as a child of God, Paul owed to the Father, Who loved him, to the Son Who died for him, and to the Spirit Who sanctified him, to cherish an undecaying, an ever growing attachment, to the cross. And this he did. He died with noble readiness for what he lived with manly devotedness. He gloried in the cross when it brought him to the scaffold. He was right; his way was as paved, and his welcome to be as sure in Heaven, as the entrance of Christ the forerunner could make them: and that was certain.

www.ingramcontent.com/pod-product-compliance
Lightning Source LLC
Chambersburg PA
CBHW070120080526
44586CB00013B/1345